AGEING IN A CONSUMER SOCIETY

From passive to active consumption in Britain

Ian Rees Jones, Martin Hyde, Christina R. Victor,
Richard D. Wiggins, Chris Gilleard and Paul Higgs

This edition published in Great Britain in 2008 by

The Policy Press
University of Bristol
Fourth Floor
Beacon House
Queen's Road
Bristol BS8 1QU
UK

Tel +44 (0)117 331 4054
Fax +44 (0)117 331 4093
e-mail tpp-info@bristol.ac.uk
www.policypress.org.uk

© The Policy Press 2008

British Library Cataloguing in Publication Data
A catalogue record for this book is available from the British Library.

Library of Congress Cataloging-in-Publication Data
A catalog record for this book has been requested.

ISBN 978 1 86134 882 1 paperback
ISBN 978 1 86134 883 8 hardcover

The right of Ian Rees Jones, Martin Hyde, Christina R. Victor, Richard D. Wiggins,
Chris Gilleard and Paul Higgs to be identified as authors of this work has been asserted by
them in accordance with the 1988 Copyright, Designs and Patents Act.

Cover design by In-Text Design, Bristol
Printed and bound in Great Britain by MPG Books, Bodmin.

Contents

List of tables and figures

Tables

Figures

Acknowledgements

This book is based on findings from an ESRC/AHRC Cultures of Consumption-funded project [RES-154-25-007]. We are very grateful to Professor Frank Trentmann, the project director, for his advice and support. We were also fortunate to have Professor Maria Evandrou and Ms Xanthippe Tzimoula who were part of the project team and we would like to thank them both for their invaluable contributions to the project.

Notes on the authors

Ian Rees Jones is Professor of Sociology at Bangor University. He has published extensively in the field of medical sociology addressing health inequalities, chronic illness and medical decision making. He is an executive committee member of the ISA RC11 (Sociology of Ageing) and his research with older people focuses on studies of early retirement and health status post-retirement. Ian currently leads an Economic and Social Research Council (ESRC)-funded research project looking at changing inequalities in health and lifestyles in later life. He is co-author with Paul Higgs of *Medical sociology and old age: Towards a sociology of health in later life* (Routledge, 2008).

Martin Hyde is a senior lecturer in sociology at Sheffield Hallam University. He was Research Fellow on the From Passive to Active Consumption study. He has worked on a number of large-scale national and international studies of later life, including the English Longitudinal Study of Ageing and the Survey of Health, Ageing and Retirement in Europe, as well as being one of the members of the original research team which designed the Swedish Longitudinal Occupational Survey of Health. His main research areas are labour market dynamics; health, leisure and consumption in later life; and global processes in later life on which he has published a number of papers in international journals. He studied at the University of Bristol.

Christina R. Victor is Professor of Social Gerontology and Health Services Research at the University of Reading. Her main research interests are in the areas of health status in later life; social networks and social relationships in later life; and with developing a population perspective on ageing and later life. She has published widely in peer-reviewed journals, has held research grants from a variety of funding sources including the ESRC and the UK Department of Health and is the author/editor of eight books in the field of ageing and later life including *The social context of ageing: A textbook of gerontology* (Routledge, 2005).

Richard D. Wiggins (Dick Wiggins) joined the Institute of Education, University of London as Head and Chair of Quantitative Social Science in 2007. His methodological interests include: the longitudinal analysis of secondary data, mixed methods, survey design, attitude measurement and sampling methodology; evaluation research; and policy analysis. Substantive research covers: the exploration of structure and agency in the context of ageing, poverty, physical and mental health and well-being, cross national differences in health and quality of life. Recently concluded research includes work under the Cultures of Consumption programme funded by the ESRC/Arts and Humanities Research Board and the ESRC's Human Capability and Resilience Network. Current activities include two new projects, 'Transitions, choices and health in later life' (New Dynamics of Ageing programme) and a cross-national study on health and poverty (Canadian Social and Humanities Research Council). He is a member of the Medical Research Council's College of Experts, an expert adviser to the Office for National Statistics' Health Variations Group and a Fellow of the Royal Society of Arts.

Chris Gilleard is the Director of Psychology and Psychotherapies for South West London and St George's Mental Health NHS Trust; he holds honorary academic positions in the Faculty of Health and Social Care Sciences, St George's University of London and Kingston University, and in the Centre for Behavioural and Social Sciences applied to Medicine, University College London. He is the co-author of two recent books addressing the changing nature of ageing and later life in contemporary Western society: *Cultures of ageing: Self, citizen and the body* (Prentice Hall, 2000) and *Contexts of ageing: Class, cohort and community* (Polity, 2005).

Paul Higgs was Principal Investigator for the From Passive to Active Consumption study. He is Reader in Medical Sociology at University College London. He is also co-author with Chris Gilleard of *Cultures of ageing: Self, citizen and the body* (Prentice Hall, 2000) and *Contexts of ageing: Class, cohort and community* (Polity, 2005). Paul has published extensively in gerontological journals in the UK and USA and was a finalist for the GSA Social Gerontology Award in 2007. He is co-author with Ian Rees Jones of *Medical sociology and old age: Towards a sociology of health in later life* (Routledge, 2008).

ONE

Social change and later life

Introduction

The study of social change has always been at the heart of the sociological enterprise and the last decades of the 20th century have provided considerable material to work on. Not only did industrialisation and urbanisation reach unprecedented levels, but the integration of the world at economic, technological and cultural levels created the globalised conditions that transformed previous experiences of international linkages (Held et al, 1999). Within these macro social processes were contained many other transformations of social life, including education, health and social care and the control of fertility. Consumption must also be included in this list, given its extending role in everyday life and popular culture. Engagement in consumption is not just the epiphenomenon of production but has also taken on a significance of its own. The diffusion of mass consumer culture, as well as the lifestyles constructed within it, is one of the most arresting features of the transformed social world in which we live.

Less noticed but of equal significance have been changes to the nature of later life. With the rise of the modern retiree, the status of old age is no longer crystallised around that of the old-age pensioner. We have seen the emergence of retirement as a significant part of the lifecourse, a period that seeks to remove itself from the residual category of discarded labour to membership of a putative leisure class (Michelon, 1954). While these changes can be framed in terms of crisis and threat regarding the future of pensions or the burden of an ageing population on health and welfare services, this kind of 'apocalyptic demography' is but one side of the equation (Gee and Gutman, 2000). As Blackburn (2002) has pointed out, the longevity revolution is rather too conveniently presented as either a dystopian crisis or a utopia of health, wealth and vitality for all. The reality is more complex, reflecting the many processes of social and cultural change associated with the transformation of work, leisure and the family as well as the broader changes in peoples' lives brought about by the rise of mass consumption.

The cohorts of people entering later life today are those who grew up in the midst of these transformations, and, perhaps more crucially, participated in their development. Earlier cohorts had entered old age with a very different (and much more limited) experience of affluence and consumer choice. Drawing on chronologies of social change, this chapter provides a background for researching the extent to which consumption is now a part of later life. It begins by focusing on the problem of studying later life in the context of rapid social change. The chapter then charts the rise of mass consumer society in the UK and how this relates to ideas of 'generational change'. Drawing on recent developments in theories of high, late or second modernity, we focus on key areas of social change and how these relate specifically to the experiences of older people in society. Following this is an overview of the rest of the book and how the various chapters reflect and relate to the central theme of consumption.

The problem of studying generations and social change

The problem of studying social change is one of distinguishing between processes of continuity, processes of readjustment and processes leading to structural changes or changes of social type (Nisbet, 1972; Abrams, 1982; Tilly, 1984; Smith, 1991). To this we would add a related difficulty – that of studying generational change. As Abrams points out, the problem of generations is a problem of mutual understanding of two different calendars: 'the calendar of the life-cycle of the individual and the calendar of historical experience' (Abrams, 1982, p 240). Researching generational change can provide an important means of understanding aspects of identity formation over time. Social theory has traditionally drawn on forms of periodisation to frame interpretations of social change. Within classical social theory, this took the form of 'before and afters'. Henri de Saint-Simon contrasted the ancient regime with the dawn of the industrial system; Alexis de Tocqueville contrasted the old regime with the new democracy, while Karl Marx and Frederick Engels wrote of the transformation from feudal to capitalist society. The drawing of contrasts between present and previous social forms can also be found in Ferdinand Tonnies' description of the shift from pre-capitalist *Gemeinschaft* to *Gesellschaft*.

All of these writers were trying to explain the shift from pre-modern to modern forms of social political and economic relations. It is this concern with modernity that unites them. However, each author conceptualised the shift differently, in part as a consequence and in part as a cause of employing different forms of periodisation. Traditional sociological accounts of modernity have, however, been criticised, both for their Eurocentrism and for ignoring the uneven nature of these changes (Latour, 1995). In response to a combination of such criticisms and the rapid social change of the past 50 years, social theorists have started to construct new frameworks for understanding modernity. Various theorists began to make reference to 'high', 'late', 'reflexive' and 'second' forms of modernity, arguing that at the heart of the post-war social transformation of 'modernity' are increasing individualisation, developments in information and communication systems and changes in the nature of capitalist relationships (Harvey, 1990; Giddens, 1991; Jameson, 1991; Beck et al, 1994, 2003). Whatever the underlying cause, there is a broad consensus among many authors that there has been a heightened sense of what Taylor (2004) refers to as the 'modern social imaginary', where individuals are more knowing and more attuned to ideas of choice, contingency and change. Outhwaite (2006) suggests that this movement towards greater individualisation and social fragmentation has led social theory to follow these transitions, refocusing, perhaps to the detriment of understanding, the sociological gaze away from institutions to organisations, from classes to strata and from politics to cultural issues.

Jessop (2002) attempts to give these transformations a more concrete foundation by focusing on the economic, political and ideological transformations that were key features of a break in the conditions of modernity occurring in the 1970s and 1980s. He charts trends towards a neoliberal, knowledge-based economy at ideological and spatio-temporal levels and in doing so suggests that in developed countries there has been a shift from the Keynsian welfare national states to Schumpeterian workfare post-national regimes. As we will see in later chapters, these shifts have profound consequences for security in later life and in terms of generational conflict over welfare resources (Esping-Andersen, 2000, 2002; Powell and Hewitt, 2002).

When seeking explanations for social and institutional change, some researchers have relied on the punctuated equilibrium model that posits long periods of stability and continuity being occasionally broken by radical change and reorganisation, this usually being accounted for in the model by some form of exogenous shock (Streeck and Thelen, 2005). Others see institutional reproduction as a dynamic process, emphasising path dependence leading to increasing returns and feedback effects (Mahoney and Rueschemeyer, 2002). Whatever the causal arguments, there is a general agreement that, following the oil price shock of the early 1970s, developed countries witnessed radical political and economic change based around processes of liberalisation, the secular expansion of market relations at nation state and global levels and the growing dominance of neoliberal ideology. These trends are contrasted with the 'golden age' of post-war capitalism, based on the post-1945 settlement that encompassed commitments to full employment, Keynsianism, recognition of trade union rights, state control of certain industries, social protection through the expansion of the welfare state, the partial decommodification of the supply of labour and an emphasis on economic growth. This so-called golden age coincided with the rise of a new 'post-1968' generation that was radicalised to fight for new social and civil rights and was also liberated from pre-existing norms.

Marwick (2003) approaches the main features of the changes that affected British society following the Second World War by constructing a periodisation based on six phases. The immediate post-war phase from 1945 to 1958 he refers to as one of 'social consensus'. The rise of affluence, permissiveness and libertarian ideas from 1959 to 1972 he refers to as 'roads to freedom'. British society turned, between 1973 and 1981, towards a 'time of troubles' characterised by conflict in Ireland, strikes and riots. The fourth phase, between 1982 and 1988, Marwick calls the 'age of privatisation, polarisation and IT', while from 1989 to 1997 he describes a society 'at odds with itself' before postulating a final sixth phase starting in 1997, which he refers to as 'restoration of consensus'. Such divisions can help illuminate social change but they may also hide more long-term continuities. While the post–war period saw the emergence, in Europe, of mass consumption, in the early 1950s many British people still lived in the cramped terrace housing of previous generations. The consumer dream was, to most people, still just a dream (Sandbrook, 2005). While youth culture was beginning to have a growing influence, Sandbrook highlights the remarkable continuity and conservatism in British life as Britain entered the consumer revolution:

> For all the novelty of Berni Inns, coffee bars and French Country Cooking, what was really remarkable about everyday life in the affluent fifties was the dogged fondness with which many ordinary people, in towns and suburbs across the country, held on to their traditional habits and hobbies. (Sandbrook, 2005, p 146)

Sandbrook is right to point out that the 1960s were dominated by youth and youth culture, although he downplays the lives of the majority who lived through that period in middle and old age in circumstances little different from those of their parents. However, in terms of the cohorts who are entering later life in the 21st century, it is their very youthfulness, exuberance and engagement with consumer culture that should be emphasised, because it is primarily the members of these cohorts who were shaped by, and who in turn a constructed, a changing habitus whose key features appear to be consumerism and a strong sense of separateness from preceding generations. It is to the key features of consumer society in the Britain of the second half of the 20th century that we now turn.

Social change and consumer society

What we recognise today as consumer society is bound closely to our understanding of modernity, which itself has complex historical roots (Sassatelli, 2007). Consumer society is based on the diffusion of commodities, goods, objects and luxury items. Historical studies of consumption have allowed us to see consumer society as more than just an effect of modern capitalism, and consumption and consumerism are not themselves the product of the industrial revolution (Fairchilds, 1993; Trentmann, 2004). What marks out modern and late modern forms of consumer society is the diffusion, proliferation and replication of styles and tastes in mass markets and commoditisation on a global scale.

Stearns (1997) has set up a periodisation of consumerism based on three stages: an early modern phase spanning the 17th and 18th centuries; a second stage of consumer growth in the late 19th and early 20th century; and a third phase of mass consumerism starting from the end of the Second World War. These distinctions are useful in acknowledging that in its earlier stages consumer and material culture was based on the sale and exchange of goods produced in small, flexible units with small, specialised distribution systems. Such forms of specialised goods can still be found, but the production and distribution of consumer goods has been transformed, first by the use of new forms of energy and the techniques of mass production during the course of the industrial revolution and, more recently, by the development of transnational systems of flexible production coupled with increasingly sophisticated and complex global distribution networks. Oldenziel and colleagues (2005) note that the range and number of consumer products such as vacuum cleaners, refrigerators and cars as well as food and lifestyle products available to mass markets have increased at a breathtaking pace. As a consequence, western societies in the late 20th century have become dominated by mass consumption. The phasing of these developments has varied within and between societies, with the greatest differences being the earlier and steeper trajectory of consumerism in the US compared with Europe (Strausser et al, 1998).

Nevertheless, the direction of travel has been constant. Britain's transformation into a mass consumer society is no exception. Analysis of consumption trends in the UK in the last quarter of the 20th century indicate a growth in non-housing expenditure and a sharp rise in spending on cars, holidays, and eating out coupled with a dramatic fall in the proportion of household expenditure spent on food, clothing and fuel (Blow et al, 2004). Equivalising for household size, those experiencing the largest growth in household spending have been couples with children (82% increase), elderly couples (58% increase) and young couples without children (57% increase). Those experiencing the lowest growth in expenditure have been single young men (21% growth) and single-parent families (16% growth). The changes in expenditure and consumption patterns of older people's households are a central focus of this book, reflecting the changes in income, wealth and transformation of the lifecourse that have occurred as a mass consumer society and its associated consumer habitus has developed.

In Britain, these developments have been accompanied by considerable economic and social change across a number of domains. These include changes in the lifecourse, in educational opportunities, in work and retirement, in household and family structures, in gender relations and in income and wealth. We will consider the lifecourse in more detail in the next two chapters, but it is useful to highlight at this point what Anderson (1985) described as the emergence of a 'normalised lifecourse' at the beginning of the 20th century. After the end of the Second World War, and particularly after the changing nature of sexual relationships in the 1960s, the destandardisation of the modern lifecourse has been hailed by a number of social theorists as a key feature of 'high', 'late' or 'second' modernity (Kohli, 1986; Bauman, 1995; Castells, 1996). Warnes (2006) described pre-war 1930s UK as a 'late industrial incipient welfare state', when the lifecourse conformed to a regular institutionalised form with comparatively short spells of education before a long period of full-time work, marriage and child rearing, culminating in a short period of retirement. By the end of the 20th century, the lifecourse had become more unstable, less constrained by the institutional frameworks of education, work and family, with longer and more variable periods of time spent in education, in work and within a fixed family structure, with longer life expectancy and earlier retirement ages. The emergence of new lifecourses, changes in the social structure, increasing individualisation and changing familial dynamics have been linked to inequalities and increasing polarisation in later life (Irwin, 1999) and to the fracturing of a monolithic social categorisation of old age and the opening up of new possibilities for later life (Gilleard and Higgs, 2000).

This period saw profound changes in the provision of primary and secondary education arising from the 1944 Education Act, which opened up new educational opportunities to working-class boys and girls. These changes were taken further with the introduction of comprehensive education and free university education in the 1960s. In 1963, there were 216,000 students in full-time higher education (including university, teacher training and further education colleges). By 1972, this figure had doubled to 457,000, reaching 1,131,000 by the end of the century (Halsey & Webb, 2000). This is of importance to cohorts entering later life at the beginning of the 20th century in two ways. First, they had greater opportunities themselves to enter and experience higher education, thus affecting career opportunities and mobility over the lifecourse and second, subsequent generations face further changes both in terms of opportunities for and funding of higher education. Furthermore, this expansion was patterned by class and gender, with a significant rise in the absolute and relative numbers of women in higher education since the mid-1960s. It should be noted, however, that despite the rising numbers of working-class entrants to higher education, their numbers remained low relative to those of the children of professional and managerial classes.

The second half of the twentieth century also witnessed considerable change in the area of work. The demise of mass working-class industries such as steel, shipping and coal led to a profound and dramatic shift in the working landscape of Britain (Grint, 1998). While recognising that this has led to considerable changes in the nature of work and work relations, it is also important to realise that there is still considerable continuity in the world of work. Findings from the Economic and Social Research Council (ESRC) Future of Work programme indicate that, despite the shift from a manufacturing economy to a more complex, post-industrial economy, class relations and divisions remain a salient and enduring part of this world of work (Taylor, 2002a). This can be clearly seen in the class differences in access to workplace benefits, with 89.9% of higher professionals/managers having an occupational pension compared with 44.4% of manual skilled and semi-skilled groups, according to the Working in Britain 2000 survey. The same survey suggests that older workers (aged 50 and over) are a key driver of British labour markets and yet there are particularly high levels of dissatisfaction among these older workers with their working conditions. Although perceptions may remain strong of older workers as contented, hard working and loyal — and indeed there is evidence to support this in terms of their low levels of absenteeism and their commitment to work – the research also suggests that a generation is emerging of 'angry and dissenting' older workers (Taylor, 2002b, p 11). Despite the clear advantages of employing older workers and the need to conform to equality legislation, the UK is still lagging behind other western countries in terms of attitudes towards older workers. From the 1980s to the beginning of this century, the employment of older workers has, with some fluctuations, remained fairly steady in the UK at around 50%. This contrasts sharply with the US and Japan, where the employment rate has been higher (around 60% in both countries) and has risen since the early 1980s. As Sennett (2006) points out, in the 'new capitalism', ageing is a domain of uselessness. This presents a paradox because although people are living longer and are healthier, prejudice in the workforce of new capitalism means workers are considered 'too old' at younger ages. The paradox becomes doubly acute when one considers the length of time individuals are likely to experience in retirement. The proportion of adult life spent in retirement in the UK, for example, has increased from under 20% in 1950 to over 30% in 2004 (Blöndal and Scarpetta, 1999; Pensions Commission, 2004). Although part of this is accounted for by a decline in the average age at exit from the labour force (from around 66 in 1950 to 63 in 2004), much of the change can be explained by the increase in life expectancy after age of exit from the workforce, which nearly doubled from 11 to 20 years over the same period.

Income levels have increased in the UK since the 1960s (Atkinson, 2000). Many of today's older people have benefited from these increases both during their working lives and in retirement. This has led to a considerable change in levels of poverty in retirement. Data from the Department of Work and Pensions based on the Family Expenditure Survey suggest that at the end of the 1970s almost 50% of individuals in pensioner families were in the bottom income quintile before housing costs. This figure had dropped to around 25% by 2004. This was accompanied by a growth in the proportion of pensioner families in the middle-income quintiles (DWP, 2006). The spread of owner occupation, the rise of single-person households, a fall in family size and the movement of women into the labour market have led to considerable changes in levels of household income and wealth. In particular, changes in women's participation and experience of paid work within the frame of greater gender equality have resulted in increasing heterogeneity in women's income in retirement (Hakim, 2000; Calasanti, 2003). Although analysis of the General Household Survey has shown that between 1973 and 1993 there was a significant increase in the earnings of women working full time relative to their husbands (Irwin, 1999), this increase has not translated fully into women's savings for pensions (Turner et al, 2004).

Since 1980 there has been a marked growth in real net pensioner income and the number of pensioners below the poverty line has fallen substantially (Hills and Stewart, 2005). Between 1979 and 1996/97, pensioners' net income rose in real terms by 64% before housing costs and by 70% after housing costs, compared with a growth of only 36% in average earnings in the whole economy

(DWP, 2006). Increases in the number of people receiving occupational pensions and increasing variability in the size of those pensions, coupled with changes in household tenure and household size and increased variation in the sources of earned and unearned income in later life, have resulted in growing income inequality within the pensionable age population. This inequality has been linked to the growth of 'high income' retirees, benefiting from substantial index-linked occupational pensions (Hills, 2004), as well as the growth in dual-earner working and dual-earner pensions – hence the rather different fortunes of pensioner couples compared with single-pensioner households.

At every stage of their adult lives, today's older people have lived through and contributed to this period of economic growth and the rise of a society based on mass consumption. They take these experiences and the material conditions accruing from these changes into later life and retirement. This book argues that we can gain a deeper understanding of the consequences this has had for later life if these changes are viewed from the perspective of being part of a wider shift in modernity – a transition towards a second modernity.

Later life and second modernity

Second modernity refers to 'the modernisation of modern society', whereby older modern structures are transformed and become contingent (Beck et al, 2003). In second modernity, there is a greater emphasis on transnational spaces where identities are plural (Bauman, 1995, 2000). Although the new tensions and conflicts that arise from these changes have been documented in the realm of work (Beck, 2000; Sennett, 2006), there is little research to address the implications of these changes for retirement and later life other than suggestions that the post-war 'golden age' of state welfare is being replaced by a 'silver age', where the welfare state is much more conscious of global competitiveness, market-based solutions and individual choice (Taylor-Gooby, 2002). The social transformations that have occurred in the post-war period have been framed in terms of the shift from organised to disorganised capitalism (Lash and Urry, 1987), the changing forms of work (Tilly and Tilly, 1998; Beck, 2000) and the disruptions that accompany the forces of globalisation (Held et al, 1999). A common theme to these and other accounts is that the decline of full employment, changes in industrial regulation and the disappearance of life-long careers have thrown institutions such as the welfare state and stable nuclear families into flux. As a consequence, social institutions become more uncertain, diffuse and changeable. So, for example, as the sexual division of labour becomes blurred, traditional gender roles and the internal dynamics of families become increasingly uncertain (Seccombe, 1993; Hakim, 2000). As the lifecourse becomes deinstitutionalised, there is greater emphasis on lifestyle and leisure in retirement (Warnes, 2006). The relatively separate and distinct lifeworlds of the immediate post-war working-class and middle-class communities have been disrupted and thrown into question by new, more self-constructed, identities (Savage, 2007).

Latour (2003) suggests that second modernity ushers in increasing uncertainty and individualisation. While the birth of the 'quasi-subject' may provide more opportunities for individuals to be authors of their own identities, the dark side of such processes may be new inclusive and exclusive practices that create new forms of inequality. In late modern consumer societies, lifestyles have become increasingly important as signifiers of status and identity (Warde, 2002). While the post-war welfare consensus provided the basis for full employment, universal health and welfare and widening educational opportunities, it also contained within it the seeds of increasing individualism, a distrust of the state and a democratisation of culture. Cohorts entering later life today have contributed to these historical transformations and carry their histories with them into the realm of old age, thus transforming old age itself. This book suggests that the ways in which these generational identities are embedded in current social phenomena have not been adequately addressed. There is a need to consider the extent to which generational forces and consumer identities are influencing the forms of social relations in later life. The material and cultural circumstances of later life have changed dramatically and one of the ways in which we can interrogate these changes is by looking at levels of engagement with consumer society.

Structure of the book

This book is based on findings from empirical research based on secondary analysis of the Family Expenditure Survey and undertaken as part of the ESRC/AHRC (Arts and Humanities Research Council) Cultures of Consumption programme (www.consume.bbk.ac.uk). It is therefore structured first around the theoretical work that informed the empirical research and then on findings in key areas of concern for later life. Finally, it addresses the implications of our findings for health and social policy as it relates to older people. Accordingly, Chapter Two begins by examining the evolution of the 'third age' in British society, tracing its rise as a concept and as a social and cultural space. Utilising demographic and historical data, the chapter presents different typologies and periodisations of the 'third age' and explores the ways in which it is expressed and reproduced in different social contexts. The literature on social change is replete with confusions surrounding the concepts of cohort, periods, generations and age. Terms such as 'baby boomers', 'sixties hippies', 'generation X' and the 'millennial generation' are often used unthinkingly. In particular, the term 'generation', although often used to refer to cohorts, retains implicit and explicit references to genealogical relationships. Chapter Three discusses the theoretical underpinnings of these concepts, drawing on the work of Mannheim (1952) and others. Having laid the ground in terms of some of the key concepts used, the book moves in the empirical sections to chart the engagement of older groups with consumer society. It is acknowledged that the evidence presented in these empirical chapters is constrained by the limitations of the data available. There is a danger therefore that engagement with consumer society is viewed through the opaque prism of household data on ownership and expenditure, leaving a limited and imperfect understanding of the experiences and meanings associated with patterns of consumption. For example, information is not included on the why, when, where and how of consumption activities. That would require a different kind of approach, focusing on the practices of older people and the uses to which they put consumer goods in everyday social relations (de Certeau, 1988). Nevertheless, the analysis presented here, based as it is on large standardised surveys of expenditure patterns, is a necessary and important first step in understanding how later life is formed by and contributes to the formation of consumer society. For example, there have been changes in household composition since the early 1970s and older households have changed in line with these secular changes. Chapter Four therefore examines the impact of these changes in household composition on consumption in later life. Following on from this, Chapter Five presents data taken from 40 years of the Family Expenditure Survey on patterns of consumption among older people in the UK from 1968 to 2003. The chapter considers the extent to which, with increasing affluence and the growth of a consumer society, the social nature of ageing has become more differentiated. Paradoxically, as later life becomes more internally differentiated, it may also become less distinct from other parts of the lifecourse. Age-specific (or appropriate) consumption and activities have diminished as retired people buy the same products and engage in many of the same activities as those in the rest of the population. Not only has the patterning of consumption and expenditure changed, but the period has also witnessed considerable changes in the patterning of inequality. Improvements in the health and wealth of the population of Britain over the 20th century have been uneven. Increasing inequalities in mortality and income since the early 1980s have been extensively documented and older people, as a group, have not escaped these trends. An important consequence is that older people can no longer be considered a residual category of society living in poverty. At the same time, there is evidence to suggest that polarisation and inequality have become acute among older age groups. Using data from the project, Chapter Six considers these changes in relation to trends in inequality and their impact on consumption patterns. One area that has been largely neglected in research on later life is that of consumption of health and health products. However, the ageing of the population has profound consequences for the healthcare industry in terms of demand for different healthcare products, consumer behaviour and marketing strategies.

Changes in government policy suggest that people at all ages will be expected to take on more responsibility in maintaining and protecting their own health (DH, 2006). The emphasis on maintaining the self is a key feature of later life in the 21st century and this will have an impact on different sections of the healthcare industry. Chapter Seven therefore delineates older people's active involvement in maintaining or improving their health through the consumption of healthcare products. The consequence of the changes to later life for health and social policy are addressed in Chapter Eight. Health and social policies have undergone considerable transformation since the early 1980s and nowhere is this more true than with respect to later life. This chapter charts the major changes and challenges to policy from the post-war era up to the present and in particular considers the implications of the rise of the citizen consumer with regard to health and social care provision. Finally, the concluding chapter argues that the role of the UK's ageing population in consumer society has been relatively neglected. The trend to earlier retirement as well as the relative affluence of many retired people is an important aspect of ageing in late modern societies. The cohorts of people retiring now are those who participated in the creation of the post-war consumer culture. These consumers have grown older but have not stopped consuming; their choices and behaviour are products of the collective histories of both cohort and generation. People approaching retirement, entering retirement or currently living in retirement will have very different experiences of later life to those of their predecessors.

TWO

The historical evolution of the third age

Introduction

The idea that later life could be represented as a third age of individual engagement and relative autonomy is one that has been contentious among social gerontologists since it started to gain widespread use in the 1990s; see Bury (1995) for a critique and Freedman (1999) for an exhortation. Part of the reason for the controversy lies not in the sentiment for a better later life but in the challenge that the idea of a third age represents for existing social gerontological theories of old age. The orthodoxy that had settled around the 'structured dependency' and political economy schools of thought focused around the idea of older people as poorly treated subjects of social policy rather than as agents enacting choices (Estes, 1979; Townsend, 1981). This view of later life was further challenged by the connections that were made, particularly in the US, between relative affluence, consumption, the pursuit of the third age and the search for 'productive aging' (Weiss and Bass, 2002). Such an approach appeared to go against many of the assumptions of social gerontology and underplayed the inequalities that exist in later life even if it was no longer possible to claim that these inequalities defined it. Moreover, the fact that the idea of the third age was being discussed at the same time as a profound restructuring of the welfare compact was occurring in both the US and UK meant that articulating such a perspective was seen as reinforcing shifts away from welfare citizenship and towards greater inequality (Estes, 2001). Consequently, the linking of old age, the third age and consumption are not only seen as problematic but also seem to undermine the generational compact between workers and retirees in the face of a changing demography. However, it is not just demography that is changing. As noted in Chapter One, the rise in post-war affluence has altered the relative fortunes of the majority of the retired population. The inequalities that exist within society are no longer structured by age but are reflected within it. As a result, an understanding of the third age and its development as a social space for later life is essential for understanding the role and significance of consumption in later life.

This chapter considers different typologies of the third age and explores the ways in which it is expressed and reproduced in different social contexts. First, the chapter addresses different conceptualisations of the third age before considering attempts to measure and identify the point of emergence of 'third age societies' and developing an argument for setting this 'emergence' in a theoretical framework that takes account of social change. The chapter then considers arguments for treating the third age as a cultural space whose size and shape varies in time and from one country to another. It concludes by considering the implications of this perspective for health and social care policy.

The third age conceptualised

In the UK, it has been Peter Laslett's (1996) vision of the third age that introduced the term into social gerontology. Heralded as the emergence of a 'new' period in the lifecourse, standing between a second age of work and a fourth age of decline and dependency, Laslett saw the third age as a phase of life offering new opportunities, freedoms and potential to the older person. He argued that retirement could usher in a new and satisfying period of life, one characterised by self-fulfilment, engagement and social worth.

While this approach has been criticised as an aspirational middle-class vision of later life (Bury, 1995), what is significant is that it does not start with a presumption that later life is itself a problem. Laslett stresses the importance of personal agency in constructing a positive third age. Although he recognises that a third age status has its structural determinants, he locates these in demographic and societal change rather than in the framework of social policy. It is the increasing life expectancy of populations that provides the underpinning for the third age, not the nature of social services. Cultural expectations are also an important determinant of the social space of later life. As Pat Thane suggests, a society's cultural representations help shape individual and collective attitudes, beliefs and responses to old age. Expectations of helplessness and dependency in later life help construct forms of dependency and contribute to the form that welfare services, both formal and informal, take (Thane, 2003). Thane suggests that demographic differences between societies influence the development of cultural aspects of ageing. She cites as example the moral panic accompanying the ageing of the population of France in the 1920s and the way this was translated into negative views of old age in France. Definitions of old age have varied throughout history, as has the significance of old age itself. The rise of the third age as a category and the disputes over its meaning need to be considered in its historical, social and cultural context.

Although Laslett did most to raise awareness of the third age, the dividing of old age into phases pre-dates Laslett's version of a third age. Thane (2000) notes that in early modern England there was a notion of a 'green old age' presaging decrepitude. In the 20th century, this became known as a distinction between young old age and old old age; a distinction that was set out formally by Neugarten (1974) in relation to old age in the American context. Differences between Laslett's conceptualisation of the third age and other European and North American understandings of the term were recognised early on by Laslett. In the second edition of *A fresh map of life* (Laslett, 1996), he was particularly critical of attempts such as those by the Carnegie Inquiry (1993, 2000) to define the third age in terms of chronological age. His criticisms have been echoed by Eric Midwinter (2005), who argues for replacing approaches to the third age based on chronological age ranges or birth dates with a 'stages of life' approach, grounded in the economic status of the citizenry (primarily related to engagement in paid work). Midwinter argues that his approach gives a more accurate picture of the relative size of first, second and third ages in the UK since the middle of the 19th century.

These definitional and conceptual differences are important because the term third age appears to be at risk of acquiring a 'taken for granted' understanding, hiding preconceived ideas about its basis and meaning. Laslett saw it as a point in the lifecourse that is both 'personally chosen' and the product of 'collective circumstances' (Laslett, 1996, p 99). This suggests that he saw it as something experienced individually in the context of a society where there is sufficient material opportunity and social disposition to act that way. Historically, he argued, it was a coming together of intellectual, cultural, economic and demographic factors. At the individual level, he was at pains to emphasise that the distinctions between first, second, third and fourth ages are often blurred within one individual's life. He gives a range of examples, including retired athletes living in the third age alongside the first age, Mozart, who might be said to have not experienced a second age at all, and Jane Austen, whom he suggests gave the appearance of living a second age when secretly she was in a third age of masterly achievement. These examples are perhaps an inevitable consequence of Laslett conceptualising the third age in terms of the 'crown of life'. In their reliance on the extraordinarily talented or lives lived in unusual circumstances, they are perhaps useful in highlighting the variability of a third-age habitus, but in so doing Laslett privileges the exceptional in defining a third age.

Laslett also sketched out a view that people 'in' the third age have a moral duty (recognised by themselves and others) as trustees of our environmental and cultural heritage. The third age should not be a period of indolence. 'The duties of those in the Third Age ...', he writes, 'include such responsibilities as the rescue of cultural institutions' (1996, p 182). This aspirational and moralising side to his work pervades his book, sitting uneasily alongside his more analytical attempts to measure the historical development of the third age.

Other formulations of the third age have been articulated. Many of these treat the third age as a 'new stage of life', characterised by a distinctly 'youthful' approach to later life, or those in the third age as members of a 'new social group' defined by their relative health and wealth. The former approach is illustrated by the 'personal growth' literature (Sheehy, 1996; Freedman, 1999), while advocates of a new socio-demographic framework promote the latter (Carnegie Inquiry, 1993). Both approaches share a common interpretation of the third age as a chronologically determined social stratum akin to terms such as 'the young elderly' or 'the young old' that had already gained currency in the work of Bernice Neugarten (1974).

An alternative version of the third age emphasises its distinctive lifestyle defined through the consumption and leisure patterns of particular cohorts of 'silver surfers', 'woopies' or 'new-agers' (Gunter, 1998). This is the province of market researchers and economists seeking to draw attention to the wealth and spending habits of retired people (Smith and Clurman, 1997; Wallace, 1999). Cultural differences are evident. While British writers such as Laslett and Young and Schuller (1991) tend to see the third age in terms of its social virtues, American writers (Weiss and Bass 2002) place more emphasis on the personal success and power associated with the third age. Americans emphasise individual lifestyle, the British social worth.

Sharing the aversion to defining the third age by retirement from paid labour are writers such as Germaine Greer and Gloria Steinem, who have written about the third age as a potentially liberating opportunity that awaits post-menopausal women (Greer, 1991; Steinem, 1994). Concentrating on the menopause rather than retirement as a marker for later life, these writers have argued that a woman's later years can be realised as an empowered lifestyle liberated from the oppression of the male gaze.

Although the chronological approach to the third age still has a following (in the UK, for example, the Economic and Social Research Council's New Dynamics of Ageing programme appears to define it as beginning at 50), other conceptualisations of the third age have taken a more individualistic approach and focused on the meanings associated with what is seen as a particular phase of the lifecycle. Weiss and Bass (2002), for example, present us with the notion of individuals in later life being able to *choose* their lifestyles:

> The life phase in which there is no longer employment and childraising to commandeer time and before morbidity enters to limit activity and mortality brings everything to a close, has been called the Third Age. Those in this phase have passed through a first age of youth, when they are prepared for the activities of maturity, and a second age of maturity, when their lives were given to those activities, and have reached a third age in which they can, within fairly wide limits, live their lives as they please, before being overtaken by a fourth age of decline. (Weiss and Bass, 2002, p 3)

This individualised approach has been taken up in the UK as well, but applied to the notion of a 'good life', so that Ball (2002), while retaining the notion of personal choice, uses the metaphor of do-it-yourself (DIY) to propose six elements for a well-lived third age: family and friends; community service and voluntary work; employment or self-employment; learning and personal development; travel and leisure activities; home and garden. Choosing well for the third age is emphasised with a similar moral tone to that adopted by Laslett, with an almost religious admonition for those who would stray on to the path of dependency:

The DIY stage of life. The greatest enemy to health, wealth and happiness is dependency; the temptation of dependency is strong for third agers, but needs to be resisted. There will be plenty of time to come to terms with it in the Fourth Age. (Ball, 2002, p 4)

Gilleard and Higgs (1998, 2000, 2005) have argued that standard accounts of ageing identities based on a socialised lifecourse with clear demarcations between adult and late adult life are becoming outdated. The previous certainties about post-working life (retirement, disengagement and old age) are disappearing, replaced by a variety of diverse lifestyles sharing a freedom secure from lack but also sharing new uncertainties, anxieties and aspirations. In this context, they see the third age as a new social field, where later life becomes more diffuse, heterogeneous and multidimensional. Seeing the third age in terms of a period or phase of life called 'the third age' becomes problematic. People entering later life can no longer be categorised en bloc as 'retirees', 'third agers' or 'pensioners'. They face a multiplicity of choices, circumstances and futures. In this sense, Gilleard and Higgs resist any attempt to construct the third age as either a demographic lifestage or biological indicator of successful ageing. Instead, they treat it as a 'cultural field', whose boundaries lie beyond any particular community of interests and belie attempts to reduce it to any particular social location based on age, class, status, race or gender. They recognise that in order for such a complex multidimensional cultural space to grow, there needs to be an open social space such that people entering later life are no longer simply differentiated by their exclusion from paid employment. Even so, the third age remains, for the time being at least, a phenomenon of the destandardised westernised lifecourse.

Measuring the third age

In attempting to chart the historical emergence of the third age, Laslett used a 'third-age indicator' (3AI) based on life tables that he combined with key economic and educational indicators to operationalise the concept of a third-age society. Calculating 3AI for a country involves using life tables to divide the number of survivors at age 70 by the number of survivors at age 25. If this ratio is greater than 0.5, Laslett claimed, a country has met the demographic criteria for the emergence of a third age. Laslett included the percentage of adults aged 25+ who are over 60 as an additional indicator that he argues needs to be at least 25% and set the economic conditions for a country to meet 3AI criteria at a minimum gross domestic product (GDP) per head of $10,000 (1996, p 118). When these conditions are met, the number of potential 'third-agers' is sufficiently large to categorise that society as having qualified as a third-age society. Figure 2.1 shows trends in 3AI for men in a range of countries during the course of the 20th century, illustrating the extent of differences in the phasing of demographic change between and within groups of developed and developing countries.

Figure 2.1: Third-age indicator trends: selected countries, 1900-2000 (men)

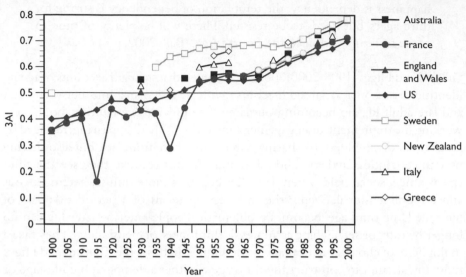

Source: Max Planck Institute for Demographic Research (www.demogr.mpg.de)

If we take these data at face value, it would appear that the UK emerged as a third-age society in the 1950s and became settled in the 1980s. Demographically, the conditions appeared earlier in places like Italy, but the economic criteria for third-age conditions would not have been met until later in the century. Indeed, Laslett acknowledged that he was unable to make firm judgements about countries like Russia, China, Japan, Greece and Poland because of the limited socio-economic data to qualify their demographic structure as third age-like. For women, the conditions of the third age do not follow Laslett's criteria well. If we apply the demographic 3AI for women, they appear to hit the criteria at a slightly earlier point in history, but there is no indication that they experienced the third age to any extent (Figure 2.2).

As noted earlier, Laslett's economic conditions for a country to meet 3AI criteria were set at the time of writing at a minimum GDP per head of $10,000. This is a figure that needs continual revising in line with inflationary pressure and economic change. Moreover, the figure does not address the distribution of resources between classes, groups and generations. Finally, Laslett's demographic approach is resolutely positivist in nature. Mannheim criticised similar positivist approaches to defining generations in the 19th century using a similar mathematical approach to calculate a generational period based on the average age at marriage (men) and half the period of marital fertility (Mannheim, 1952).

Despite the conceptual and methodological problems of his demographic approach, Laslett was able to chart some of the demographic and economic changes that provide conditions within which a third age can develop. It is clear that since the 1970s in western countries, more people are experiencing longer

Figure 2.2: Third-age indicator trends: selected countries, 1900-2000 (women)

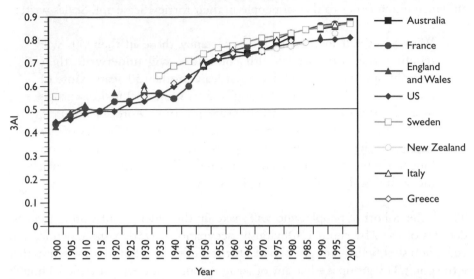

Source: Max Planck Institute for Demographic Research (www.demogr.mpg.de)

retirement, with higher material wealth and greater opportunities for consumption and leisure. The third age has demographic and social facets, but it can also be related to differential patterns of economic, political and cultural change. In North America, the third age developed earlier and has assumed greater importance because of economic and cultural change. Greater media attention to the rising affluence, better health and longer life of older people itself facilitates the formation of a third age. Not only do people have to have longer life expectancy and more opportunities in retirement, but they also have to be aware of this fact. There is a sense of attitudes being important as well as appropriate cultural and educational facilities being available. This in turn is a product of the media and the market.

Is the third age really a matter of personal choice? A growing body of evidence suggests that income determines patterns of consumption and lifestyle more than age. As Cook and Settersten point out, 'level of resources is an important determinant of the choices people are able to make and the needs they are able to meet' (Cook and Settersten, 1995, p 21). Since the late 1980s, several reports point to the changing circumstances of retired people. Michael Hurd has written:

> During most of history to be old was to be poor. This is certainly no longer the case in the United States. On average the elderly appear to be at least as well off as the non-elderly and possibly better off. (Hurd, 1989, p 663)

Other economic commentators have emphasised the unevenness of this improvement in economic status. But what is most distinct is the emergence of cohorts who, in their late fifties and sixties, express lifestyles and possess a level of affluence much closer to that of people in their forties. Scase and Scales write:

> With an overall increase in life expectancy, those in their 50s will redefine 'age'. Improved health conditions will underwrite their assumptions that they will live for at least another 30 years. More of them will see themselves as 'young' and be more inclined to engage in a diversity of active, creative leisure pursuits. More self-focused, hedonistic attitudes will emerge as they imitate the lifestyles of the young. ... there is evidence to suggest that age, in itself, is now no longer *the* predictor of spending, saving and consumption pattern. (Scase and Scales, 2000, p 1, emphasis in original)

This is the cohort of people who will make up the older population in the first decades of the 21st century. Obviously, occupational work history, gender and education stratify this group, much like the rest of society, but in some senses that is the point. This group is – like any other age group in society – stratified. Though little systematic longitudinal work has been done on the nature of income and consumption pre- and post-retirement (Barker and Hancock, 2000), what has been done indicates an increasing equivalence between pre- and post-working net incomes (Casey and Yamada, 2002; Yamada, 2002; Hungerford, 2003).

If the third age exists, how is it realised? Gilleard and Higgs (2005) identify class, cohort and community as key elements in illuminating the field of the third age. Class is important because it reflects the linkages between the economy and the conditions of living in later life. Cohort is important because it highlights the importance of generations and period in the structuring of the third age. Community is seen as important because its transformation from the normative structures of the neighbourhood to the symbolic relations of identity and lifestyle facilitates the opening up of new social spaces.

Evandrou and Falkingham (2000) have pointed out how much of our understanding of old age is derived from cohorts who were born in the 1910s whose experiences across the lifecourse differ markedly from those born a generation later in the 1940s. The first cohort of 'baby boomers' is starting to retire. In terms of access to resources, women in these new cohorts of retirees have greater work participation rates and are much more likely to have worked full time prior to retirement. Men (and women, though to a lesser degree) have benefited from access to occupational pensions. Couples have benefited from being part of dual-earner families and from the rise in home ownership. Evandrou and Falkingham conclude that the baby-boom cohorts are likely to be 'better off in retirement than today's older people' (Evandrou and Falkingham, 2000, p 34). Rather than attempting to measure the third age, attention should be given to the historical periodisation of its emergence and the circumstances under which it has flourished.

Periodisation and the third age

In an attempt to provide a clear definition of periodisation, Gerhard (1973) identified three main types: *chronological*, referring to the counting of centuries or years marking beginning and ends of eras (for example, the Christian era); *evolutionary*, referring to a period as a phase in development (for example, slavery, feudalism, capitalism); and *meaning*, referring to attempts to summarise the essence of an age (for example, the roaring '20s). What is common to all three is the goal of clarifying processes and events, identifying continuities and discontinuities and thus facilitating interpretation. At the epistemological level, periodisation is a social construct that arises from abstracting from historical sources based on criteria defined by the sociologist or historian. As such, periodisations have the same definitional problems as any variable and can overlap depending on the different criteria being used to define them. One form of periodisation that has become fashionable in recent years is that associated with the idea of generational change. Jason Scott Smith (1998) notes a tendency for 'generational thinking' that tends to confuse personal experience with social change. The origins of this is traced to the cohort of people born in the 1880s and 1890s who experienced the full horror of the Great War and who tended to identify their own histories with that of world history. Such a 'generational identity' was highlighted by Mannheim (1952) and has been used by numerous social historians since (Strauss and Howe, 1992, 1997). The tendency to focus on the decade as a marker of generational identity, though seductive, has a number of implications. There is a sense of time speeding up and of an increasing emphasis on, or search for, discontinuity. There is also an increasing obsession with personal histories and increasing yearning and nostalgia for the recent experienced past (Hazlett, 1998). The decade becomes a category based on culturally shared events that tend to equivalise units of time while ignoring or underplaying the long duree of social, political and historical forces. Examples include the perceived 'normalcy' of the 1950s (the 'Ovaltiney generation'), the radical upheaval of the 1960s and the self-centredness and malaise of the 1970s. Presenting periodisation in such simplistic terms can mean we miss more important long-term social phenomena such as the decline in manufacturing in the UK economy and the rise and fall of trade union membership. As Gerhard (1973) argues, we may have to periodise, but we ought to have meaningful periods.

Jessop (2002) distinguishes periodisation from other historical methods such as chronicles, narratives or genealogies. Chronologies use unilinear timescales to order actions and events, while periodisation adopts a more complex approach utilising several timescales to order events in terms of trends or cycles. While a chronology is a grouping of events in successive stages to provide simple narrative explanations, periodisation classifies events according to their conjunctual implications to provide an explanatory framework. Jessop argues that there are ontological, epistemological and methodological aspects to this. At the ontological level, without social change periodisation would be meaningless. On the other hand, if everything continually changed, periodisation would become impossible. Periodisation is meaningful therefore where relative continuity means that a particular period's structural coherence is not disrupted and discontinuity leads to sufficient disruption of one structural set leading to the formation of another.

Others (Lieberman, 2001; Katznelson, 2002; Jones, 2003) emphasise the need to test ideas about causation using clear periodisation strategies. These are summarised as processes of *simplification* (through identifying events and/or processes as points of rupture, division, cut-offs or dividing lines for a chronology) and/or *boundary setting* (periods have boundaries that contain important events, turning points that are conceptualised as the markers of variations in explanatory variables). These 'moments', as Lieberman calls them, include wars, revolutions, elections and crises. In Chapter One, key elements of the social changes experienced in the UK since the early 1960s were identified and linked to the rise of mass consumer society. These included rising incomes coupled with increasing income inequality, improvements in the income levels of older people, increasing educational opportunities, changes in gender relations at work and in the private sphere and changes in household structure. Specifically in the UK case, they include the formation of the welfare state, a period of austerity immediately following the Second World War before the cultural transformations experienced from the 1960s onwards. After the economic and industrial conflict of the late 1970s, the election of the Thatcher government heralded a period of aggressive monetarism, high unemployment, recession and public expenditure cuts. From the mid-1980s onwards, the price of oil began to fall and financial deregulation and privatisation continued apace. In the early 1990s, economic recession co-existed with rapid technological change. The election of a Labour government in 1997 coincided with a period of sustained economic growth, although inequalities in income persisted. Evandrou and Falkingham (2000) have linked the dates of such key events to the ages of particular cohorts. Table 2.1 presents an adaptation of this work outlining the key phases of social change in the post-war period experienced by particular cohorts that have entered or are about to enter later life. The table gives an indication of the extent to which cohorts now entering later life and approaching retirement experienced the rise of consumer society at early stages in their lives and how the rise of consumer society coincided with other key changes and processes that contribute to the construction of habitus that these cohorts take with them into later life.

The third age as a cultural space

The periodisation sketched out above suggests that the third age is more than just a code for 'well-off retired people'. The reflexive characteristics that Laslett attributes to the third-ager – the knowing and deliberate cultivation of a retirement lifestyle – are not simply the product of having the resources to indulge in consumerism.

Table 2.1: Age of selected birth cohorts at the time of other economic and cultural events

	Year	Event	Birth cohort			
			1920	1935	1947	
Welfare state	1944	Education Act	24	9		
	1945	First shipment of bananas to UK after Second World War	25	10	1	
Austerity years	1948	NHS, transistor radio invented	28	13	7	
	1954	Clothes rationing ends	34	19	7	
	1955	Commercial TV starts in Britain (Gibbs SR toothpaste)	35	20	8	
'You've never had it so good'	1957	Consumers' Association and *Which?* magazine	37	22	10	
	1961	Oral contraceptive launched	41	26	14	
	1963	Cassette tape recorder	43	28	16	
	1967	Abortion Act, homosexual acts between consenting men legalised, free contraception on NHS, first colour TV in Britain	47	32	20	
1970-73 boom years	1971	1969 Divorce Reform Act implemented, decimalisation of coinage	51	36	24	
	1972	Home video games	52	37	25	
1974-75 oil crisis	1974	International Monetary Fund assists Britain	54	39	27	
	1975	Equal Pay Act and Sex Discrimination Act implemented, SERPs (state earnings-related pensions) established, personal computers introduced	55	40	28	
	1979	Margaret Thatcher elected, removal of exchange controls	59	44	32	
	1982	Unemployment over 3 million; Falklands War, CDs go on sale	62	47	35	

(continued)

Table 2.1: Age of selected birth cohorts at the time of other economic and cultural events (continued)

	Year	Event	Birth cohort		
			1920	1935	1947
	1984	Privatisation of British Telecom	64	49	37
	1986	'Big Bang' deregulation of the Stock Exchange	66	51	39
1988-92 recession	1987	'Black Monday' on the Stock Exchange	67	52	40
	1990	ANC activist Nelson Mandela freed, poll tax riots, Germany reunified, invasion of Kuwait, Thatcher resigns	70	55	43
	1991	World Wide Web, Soviet Union dismantled, NHS reform	71	56	44
	1993	Maastricht Treaty ratified	73	58	48
1993 recovery	1994	National Lottery	74	59	47
	1997	Labour government elected, Independent Bank of England, Government White Paper (*A new partnership for care in old age*)	77	62	50
	2001	9/11	81	66	54
	2003	Iraq War, last commercial flight of Concorde	83	68	56

Source: Adapted from Evandrou and Falkingham (2000)

There have, after all, always been rich old people. What distinguishes the third age is its emergence from a set of particular historical and cultural processes to which different cohorts have been differentially exposed during the course of their adult lives. Giddens (1991) has focused on the commodification of lifestyle in late modern society, pointing out how people's consumption of commodities is central to the construction of 'narratives of the self' and the formation of social identity. To this we can add that consumerist lifestyles are no longer the product of conspicuous consumption located within a small band of increasingly affluent older people (Veblen, 1953). Rather, they connect to a broader transformation of the cultural sphere arising from capitalist developments of the commodity form (Lee, 1993). Purchasing decisions are made not to express one's wealth, but to express an engagement with modern life. While the two processes are intertwined, it is the change in emphasis, the dominance of style over substance, that characterises patterns of consumption in the post-war period.

Bauman (1998) goes so far as to argue that the 'aestheticisation' of consumption has replaced the work ethic as the most consistent aspect of people's lives. Consumption presents individuals with the means of understanding contemporary life as well providing a set of moral underpinnings. The periodisation set out in this chapter illustrates the extent to which people at or reaching retirement age today have lived most of their adult lives exposed to and participating in an expanding consumer market. Evidence of their increasing material and symbolic participation in modern life can be found readily enough in surveys of the ownership of consumer durables among retired people's households (ONS, 2002b, p 157; 2002c, p 48). The following chapters will attempt to add meat to the bones of this evidence by looking at the British case in detail. However, it is suggested at this point that it is the consumption of the products of mass culture and the exposure to mass media that most distinguish the contemporary leisure activity among the retired population.

While Giddens (1991) drew attention to the increasing reflexivity of late modern society that contributes to 'projects of the self', Laslett also referred to the significance of reflexivity in contemplating one's old age as a feature not previously evident in the lives of older people (Laslett, 1996). Evidence of a growing concern over ageing as a personal fate is not hard to find. What is significant about this late modern concern with ageing is not simply a fear or distaste towards old age but its problematic status; problematic because there is now the possibility of other ways of living that do not constitute 'old age'. As Featherstone and Hepworth (1998) point out:

> It is precisely in the struggle to reconstruct this cultural inheritance of pessimism that the element of difference between past and present attitudes towards ageing through the later period of the life course may be found. (p 150)

Explicit in Laslett and implicit in several other writers is the importance of choosing the 'correct' life, in effect employing effective 'technologies of the self'

(Foucault, 1988) to be successful in retirement. It is not enough simply to choose; one must also choose wisely (Bauman, 1995).The ideology of the third age meshes with concerns about the future of the welfare state's relationship to the retired and the old.The issues prompted by Laslett's demographic transition are seen not as an opportunity for third-agers, but as a policy problem for modernisers. If the history of the welfare state has been inextricably linked to that of old age (Higgs, 1995), the modernisation now on offer focuses on changing the relationship.

The argument for equality of all in old age advocated by those connected with the structured dependency position (Townsend and Walker, 1995) seems increasingly anachronistic. Giddens (1994, 1998) argues that the era of the welfare state does not chime with the agency required to deal with the risks created by reflexive modernisation, adding that it is only by abandoning the connection between ageing and welfare that old age can become free of the structured dependency described by so many authors.While the position advanced by Giddens has many shortcomings, one thing seems to be true – that no serious attempts are being made to strengthen the link between the welfare state and later life.

If a case can be made for the existence of a non-normatively based idea of a third age, what consequences follow from this? How does this affect our understanding of ageing? It can be argued that where the existence of the third age matters most is the implicit division it creates for those excluded from it.This is an issue that Laslett effectively ignores but that has profound consequences for the experience of old age.Although Laslett identified a 'fourth age' of decrepitude, he was perhaps too fixated on the idea of the 'compression of morbidity' to take seriously the significance politically as well as culturally of such a designation. It is as if Laslett aspired to take the body out of the equation of ageing and, in so doing, forgets that the ageing body retains a key significance that cannot be ignored. Laslett's idea of the third age created the conditions for a fundamental social dichotomy between a third and fourth age.This dichotomy is already in evidence in cultural terms and through its realisation by the state in terms of its health and social policies. The move in social policy towards consumer empowerment and voice is based on the assumption of users as capable of articulating their interests; that they have agency. This becomes problematical for those who become frail or dependent as proxies and advocates are created to shape a voice for the voiceless and exercise power on behalf of the powerless.

The consequence is that those unable to participate in the third age are seen as at risk of falling out of the discourses of the modern world into the virtual reality of public service consumers. Such attributional communities ensure in practice that they become objects of discourse rather than subjects of their own decisions. In a world that increasingly emphasises the importance of personal responsibility in all things, such 'discourses of activism' push those deemed to have entered the fourth age into a social space lacking any opportunity or scope for individual reflexivity. Some social gerontologists seek to show that there is a continuum of interest between third and fourth agers (Bengston and Putney, 2006). However, the third and the fourth age are not commensurate social spaces, nor are they dialectically related identities. The social cultural and historical processes governing the third age are quite different from those that govern the fourth. We may purchase long-term care insurance, but this is not because we want long-term care.

Conclusion

Laslett assumed that the third age would be realised through the individual agency of social actors under conditions of improved human capital. It would be supported by a moral economy, deriving little of its substance from a material base but still located in a normative order of age appropriateness and reciprocity. Exhortation to choose and choose wisely was deemed sufficient and necessary to sustain and develop a third-age culture. The threat, if any, arose from individual indolence and ill health. The above discussion points to a different conclusion. The third age is neither an identity nor a possession. Rather, as Gilleard and Higgs (2000) have argued, it is a cultural field, whose dynamic derives from consumption and whose boundaries are tied to the historical changes that provided the context for its gestation. It is underpinned by the post-war transformations in the nature of global capitalism, in cumulative improvements at all ages, and, particularly in later life, in health, wealth and happiness (Manton and Gu, 2001; Yamada, 2002; Spillman, 2004; Äijänseppä et al, 2005; Yang, in press) alongside a series of cultural transformations connected to the generational habitus born in the 'long '60s'. Whatever exhortations are made to a sense of social responsibility and community mindedness, the sustainability of the third age seems dependent on an expanding global capitalism and the consumer culture it promotes.

THREE

Cohort, generation and time

Introduction

The horizontal divisions within society, such as cohort, age group and generation, have had considerably less attention paid to them than the vertical divisions of class, gender and ethnicity. This may reflect the starker social polarisation that emerged during the course of industrialisation, a polarisation that preoccupied the founders of the emergent social sciences. Horizontal divisions within society may have been recognised but they were not seen as so significant, or as key sites of social conflict. While there is still continued debate regarding the nature and significance of many of the vertical divisions in society, the importance of horizontal divisions has become more prominent. Indeed, some writers now argue that in contemporary society, generation is replacing class as the key site of contemporary social conflict (Turner, 1989; Becker, 1991). All of this makes it important to clarify the different but related horizontal divisions reflected in terms such as 'age group', 'stage of life', 'cohort', 'period' and 'generation'.

Erdman Palmore (1978) pointed out that in most social science research, the need to separate age effects from period and cohort effects is inescapable. Not only are there ageing processes and issues of human development to deal with, but differences between generations and trends over time potentially confound any interpretation based on chronological age. While Palmore argued that it is always important to measure all three types of difference, doing so has always been a problem. Chronological age at least has the virtue of being an ordinal value, even though what a particular age may mean is historically contingent. Period, as has been seen in Chapter Two, is more contentious, as is the idea of generation, since both rely on interpretation. Even the idea of cohort, which seems straightforward, depends for much of its meaning on its conflation with generational effects.

These issues are highlighted in any consideration of the use of the term 'generation'. Two approaches dominate the conceptualisation of this problem. The first is associated with the demographer Norman Ryder, who argued that 'cohort' was a more 'neutral' concept for understanding the interplay between history and biography than terms such as generation. He defined cohort as 'that aggregate of individuals who experienced the same event within the same time interval ... [where typically] the defining event has been birth' (Ryder, 1997, p 68). For Ryder, cohort represents 'a proxy measure for what are in fact traits, dispositions and behaviours and ... the social relationships in which [they] are embedded, that actually carry the "effect" and provide theoretically meaningful interpretation' (Hardy and Waite, 1997, p 6). Seeking to bring methodological clarity to the study of social change, Ryder argued that cohort should serve as the lens through which other, more deterministic, processes of social change can be observed. While helping to focus attention on the distinct experiences of a particular generation, 'cohort' remained, for Ryder, an analytic tool to uncover processes whose understanding lay elsewhere.

The second approach emphasises the cultural distinctiveness of 'generations' as a way of linking history and biography. This is the approach associated particularly with the German sociologist Karl Mannheim. In his seminal paper on the 'problem of generation', Mannheim wrote that the term 'generation' contained two related and essential elements (Mannheim, 1952). The first refers to a common location in historical time (generational location); the second to a distinct consciousness of that historical position, a 'mentalité' or 'entelechie'[1] formed by the events and experiences of that time (generational style). Both location and consciousness are necessary elements, in Mannheim's formulation, in order that 'generation' can function as a structuring process on a par with the vertical structures of class and gender. This places an emphasis on what Ryder was critical of, namely giving the idea of generation an endogenous (some might say 'mythical') significance and making it appear to be a vehicle of social change. Instead, Ryder wanted to treat 'generation' as a form of social categorisation whose explanatory power derives primarily, if not exclusively, from its role as a 'surrogate ind[ex] for the common experiences of many people in each category' (Ryder, 1997, p 72).

Mannheim's position, although a point of departure for many writers, did not lead to any resolution of the problem of generation. Kertzer has argued that Mannheim's difficulty was confounding the genealogical meaning of generation (the age-related link between parents and children) with two other distinct phenomena, namely cohort (a population sharing a common historical origin, typically a shared year of birth) and historical period or era (a common set of historically determinate experiences) (Kertzer, 1983). The solution for Kertzer was to confine 'generation' strictly to its usage as a term for parent–child relationships and use 'cohort' to represent a population sharing a common historical experience by virtue of sharing a common year of birth. These and many similar injunctions have fallen on deaf ears. The contemporary use of the term 'generation' retains its allegorical linkage with systems of intra-familial transmission and the reproduction of the domestic household. It also retains the sense of a shared historical consciousness, so central to the experience of continuity and change in modernity and, of course, it frequently substitutes for 'cohort'. Despite its 'waffly' status (Abrams, 1970), the Mannheimian concept of generation has persisted within the social sciences. It possesses a resonance that cannot be easily ignored.

Social change and generation

The earliest concerns of the classical sociologists such as Comte, Durkheim and Marx focused on historical periodisation rather than age or cohort. For them, there was only one really important 'transition', namely the emergence of modern urban industrial society from its predecessors, however categorised. The notion of a society undergoing 'revolutions' in its social relations and systems of symbolic exchange began to be articulated from the latter half of the 19th century. This focus on change, however, concentrated primarily on the origins of this change and the 'new' characteristics of 'modern society'. During the 20th century, the focus changed and the time frame shortened. Change was to be reckoned more in decades than in centuries. The greater differentiation of culture by cohort experiences (the multiplication of generational units, to use Mannheim's terminology) and the compression of generational time into ever-narrower periodisations led to a greater segmentation of modernity. The sensitivity to and desire for change expressed in a self-aware 'modernism' became ever more intense.

By the late 1960s, generational lifestyles, capable of enduring 'beyond the bounds of age spans, age groups and, in principle, the life cycle' were seen as having replaced, or being about to replace, previous forms of social identity (Abrams 1970, p 183). When Philip Abrams made this suggestion, he still assumed that these new generational lifestyles would be presaged on a shared political world view, albeit fashioned by a distinct 'post-war' outlook. Others proposed similar broad changes in generational world views based on the full realisation of modernity as society moved from conditions of scarcity to those of a new post-scarcity. Inglehart, for example, sought to demonstrate the existence of an inter-generational shift in values. He saw this shift as representing a move from those concerned with, and fashioned by, the need for material security that pre-occupied cohorts born before the depression of the 1930s, to 'post-materialist' issues, such as personal liberty and self-expression, that have preoccupied cohorts born since (Inglehart, 1997). Others have emphasised the mass expansion of 'surplus' or 'decorative' consumption as a key source of generational differentiation that was first epitomised in the lifestyle youth movements of the 1960s (Murdock and McCron, 1976; Hebdidge, 1979). Given the many sources that can serve as a base for what Mannheim had called 'generational consciousness', the principal question that this chapter addresses is how 'generation' should best be understood. This question, we shall argue, can only be addressed by considering how historical periods are expressed and realised within individual lifecourses, for it is through the interaction between cohorts and periods that generations emerge.

The social meaning of a generation

Raymond Williams has argued that 'the modern sense of generation in the ... sense of a distinctive kind of people or attitudes ... only fully develop[ed] from the mid-nineteenth century' (Williams, 1983, p 140). According to Williams, the new cultural and intellectual sensibilities that began to emerge during this time fostered a developmental approach to history that became the study of how society was moving towards the realisation of a socially progressive future. 'Generation' was imbued with an added significance as being both the 'carrier' of and the 'arena' where these new cultures established themselves. Consciousness of generation went hand in hand with consciousness of humanity's capacity for social revolution. For Williams, 1848 was a watershed. After the revolutionary events of that year, 'generation' could no longer 'unthink itself' back to a mere cyclical biological process. It had achieved a 'conscience collective' and thereby became a potential social and political institution.

'Generational cohort analysis' has flourished within the field of 'political' sociology (Cutler, 1977). Here the approach has been to draw boundaries around birth cohort groups and link these boundaries to putatively iconic 'moments' in history that thus define the generation. Analyses of differences between these event-bounded birth cohorts are used to examine secular changes in socio-political attitudes. Writers have varied in the extent to which they have emphasised each cohort's generational location (Cutler, 1977) or its shared consciousness (Schuman and Scott, 1989). Only among the latter group of researchers has serious thought been given to identifying the boundaries of a 'generational style'. Harrison White has argued that 'cohorts only become [social] actors when they cohere enough around events ... to be called generations' (White, 1992, p 31). He defines generation as 'a joint interpretive construction which insists upon and builds among tangible cohorts defining a style recognized from outside as well as from inside itself' (White, 1992 p 32). White argues that generation is a cohort's consciousness of itself – conscious of what it is and how it differs from other cohorts. By drawing attention to this consciousness of difference, White raises, but does not solve, the issue of boundaries as well as the means by which generational or cohort boundaries can be constructed.

In response to 'the problem of the historical constitution of generations as collective identities', Michael Corsten suggests (Cortsen, 1999, p 250) that generations acquire a sense of collective identity within 'cultural circles', which he defines as common and distinct forms of discourse and social practice. The concept of 'cultural circles' has potential heuristic value, but Corsten fails to give it real purchase by leaving open the question of how any generation goes about articulating its generational consciousness and how a generation forms its cultural circles. For there to be a generational consciousness (or identity or lifestyle, the issue remains the same) there needs to be events or practices located in time that shape the discourses that set the boundaries of the generational field.

Most research in this area has focused on public events. Henk Becker (1991) has tried to develop empirical tests of generational boundaries in his examination of Dutch social change in the post-war era. Like Corsten and other supporters of Mannheim's position, Becker argues that 'generation' is taking over from 'social class' as the major dynamic of social change in the post-war period:

> ... as soon as society moves toward openness, specific generations become institutionalised and partially take over the role of social classes as arrangements for the allocation of opportunities [and] the distribution of scarce goods. (Becker, 1991, pp 221-2)

Exposure to key historical events that take place during each cohort's transition to adulthood provides the markers for each generational field. Becker argues that there have been five key 'events' that have defined the generational identities of post-war cohorts in Dutch society (the Depression, the Second World War, the post-war labour boom, the 'cultural revolution of the 1960s' and the 1970s' 'recession'). Birth cohorts growing up within each of these periods have been shaped into a generation by the unique influence of these events during their transition to adulthood. Although Becker acknowledges processes of continuous change, such as expanding educational provision, developments in the labour market and the transformation of the position of women, he gives less significance to them.

A major problem with Becker's approach is that he equates specific historical events with social changes that extend beyond the events themselves and are not contained by them. The collective identity of a generation, one that is actively felt and articulated by members of that generation, and one that structures their actions as social agents, cannot be generated by borrowing from history and ascribing from that an identity. A better definition of a generation's 'cultural circle' is needed than one based on simply living through particular historical events.

Vincent (2005) also focuses on the significance of social events in his account of the generational consciousness of those people in Britain who lived through the Second World War as children and who constitute a 'war generation'. However, he also argues that 'generations are emergent cultural phenomena associated with common economic interests' that manifest themselves in political behaviour (Vincent, 2005, p 596). As a consequence, the war generation is defined more by its past than its present.

By focusing on selected socio-political events as Becker, White, Vincent and others such as Edmunds and Turner (2002) have done, an appearance of precision is established that places the onus on the 'event' or 'period' to confer an 'identity-generating' meaning. The translation of an historical event into the collective identity of a generation is then given a determining role in social change. One could just as easily omit the central term. What happens then is social history, not sociology.

In order for the advocates of a 'generational approach' to advance their case, they need to define the nature of generational identities and the means by which they function without relying on the privileging of 'critical events'. Cultural identities may incorporate historical events in defining a shared history, as Benedict Anderson (1988) has argued in his account of the 'imagined community' of the nation. However, such signifiers are typically established retrospectively and their relationship to current social realities is iconic rather than experientially formative in the way that students of political generations seem to claim (Cutler, 1977).

Generational identities and the cultural turn

Attempts at empirical pattern analysis based on the juxtaposition of certain birth cohorts with certain historical events do not provide a satisfactory delineation of a 'generation cohort' as a social identity, let alone as a potential structuring structure. What other methodologies might? As has been pointed out, much of the work seeking to provide an empirical delineation of 'generation' has come from political sociology. An alternative approach is that drawn from cultural studies, with its emphasis on ideas of 'identity' and 'difference'. Events and episodes in history impinge on individual lives in many complex ways, but what is noteworthy about the 20th century is the extent to which those events are processed through the media, whose interpretation of the events provides the dominant cultural or symbolic frame of reference. As local communities have declined in significance, shared access to and shared meanings of public events have been provided by a public media whose audience is much broader than a local or even national community. Arguably, it is the mass culture established by the media (radio, TV, film and, most recently, the internet) that creates the cultural circles that Corsten (1999) suggests shape generational consciousness. This is not to dismiss the impact of key events and historical processes; rather, it emphasises the crucial importance of continuities and discontinuities in material conditions that structure the formation of circuits of cultural capital.

Shifting attention from political sociology to cultural studies, alternative approaches to conceptualising 'generation' become possible. Specifically, by adapting Bourdieu's concepts of 'habitus' and 'field'[2], generation becomes not so much an aggregate of individuals born at a certain time, but a cultural field emerging at a particular moment in history, distributed through a new mass culture (Gilleard and Higgs, 2005). Such a cultural field shapes and is shaped by the particular tastes, values and dispositions of those cohorts whose interpretations of the world have been most influenced by mass culture. This allows Mannheim's concept of a generational location to be redefined as a generational 'field', characterised by the emergence of a changed relationship between past and present social spaces. Generational style or consciousness is treated, in like fashion, as a generational 'habitus' – a set of dispositions that generate and structure individual practices that emerge and are defined by the forces operating within a particular generational field. Such an interpretation accords well with Bourdieu's own work on 'generations', when he stated that:

> ... generational conflicts oppose not age classes separated by natural properties but habitus which have been produced by different modes of generation ... which ... cause one group to experience as natural and reasonable practices or aspirations which another group finds unthinkable or scandalous. (Bourdieu, 1977, p 78)

As Bourdieu points out, habitus are not the expressions of 'any intentional calculation or conscious reference to a norm' but the products of a 'systematicity' within the objective circumstances surrounding a social group or class that are 'laid down in each agent by his earliest upbringing' (Bourdieu, 1977, pp 80-1). In other words, it is the links that exist within the discourse and practices of a particular group that reveals the habitus, rather than the individuals' reflections on their actions. Habitus are thus derived from, but not defined by, the distinctive actions of particular people in particular settings or fields. A key aspect of Bourdieu's work was his focus on distinction as a way of articulating cultural power, a line of thought that brings habitus back to a concern with the organisation of difference and a way for lifestyle to connect with generation as both an organising principle as well as a source of social differentiation.

Gilleard and Higgs (2005) stress the distinction between 'generation' and 'cohort', with the former representing a distinct, temporally located cultural field within which individuals from a variety of overlapping birth cohorts participate as generational agents. This they distinguish from a view of a generation as a birth cohort whose identity is defined by exposure to a specific event or set of 'socialising' events. Greater or lesser 'access' to the sources of power operating within a cultural field differentiates one cohort from another. Crucially, the degree of such participation will structure the depth and breadth of the habitus that members of particular cohorts and hence age groups form.

Gilleard and Higgs argue that there are three advantages of formulating 'the problem of generation' in this way. First, it avoids the problem of a conflation between age groups, cohorts and periods, whereby each is defined as the product of the other two. As has been pointed out by many earlier writers, because each of these terms is treated as being constituted out of the other two, no distinct explanations can be made for one element without it being equally determinate for the others (Palmore, 1978). Treating generation as a cultural field avoids defining it by reference to the membership of a specific cohort. Second, such an approach enables actors to be treated as individuals who will inevitably vary in their level of engagement with emerging and established generational fields. Each individual member of a birth cohort need not serve as a 'representative' of this or that generation, but the generational field is defined through the pattern of linkages between different lifestyle practices. Third, this approach recognises the importance of changing material conditions that structure the symbolic exchange that mediates such patterns of engagement, enabling a focus on the motors that drive the new circuits of cultural capital. In other words, it fosters a form of *historical materialism* in explicating the formation and maintenance of each generational field.

Historical periods and generational boundaries

Gilleard and Higgs (2005) identify the 1960s as the key period that shaped the generational habitus of the third age, with its emphasis on choice, autonomy, self-expression and pleasure. Their argument seeks to privilege this period as making salient within the new mass society of post-war western society a powerful horizontal division in the cultures of the three worlds (Denning, 2004). The cultural significance of the 1960s stands in marked contrast to the undifferentiated decades immediately before and after it. Many aspects of the third age, Gilleard and Higgs claim, have their origins in the mass consumption established within post-war 'youth culture'. The confounding of the 'decorative' aspects of youth culture (Hebdidge, 1979) with the more substantive shift towards consumption that was taking place at that time has led many to equate lifestage with consumption. The result is that 'youthfulness' has become associated with consumption and 'age' with the failure to participate in consumer culture. This association is one that we seek to unravel and challenge in this book.

The effects of post-war youth culture are no longer confined to the practices of people of a particular age. Their habitus have spread across the lifespan in what one author has called 'the teen-aging of modern culture' (Danesi, 2003). Nevertheless, the origins of the third age reflect the circumstances and experiences that specifically affected the youth of a particular era. Three features are noteworthy: the centrality of mass consumption oriented towards pleasure and leisure; an acute antagonism between youth and age, the new versus the old; and the privileging of a disembedded individualisation with its politicisation of the personal. Youth culture was a defined set of practices that engaged teenagers and young men and women at all levels of society. It privileged practices that were dependent on, but not confined within, the expanding fields of retail capital. As Capuzzo has pointed out, 'young people as a uniform category without significant internal differences reappeared in the … 1950s … as the product of an attempt to build a new market – in other words, a commercial and media creation' (Capuzzo, 2001, p 156). But youth culture was more than a media creation. It was a field in which young people themselves exercised a growing influence. It was the systemic inter-relationships between the actions, discourse and consumption of young people that helped found the generational field that would come to situate the third age as a distinct, lifestage-associated, cultural field of particular salience to those growing up and growing older during this period.

As these inter-relationships grew more established within people's lives, they incorporated a wider range of practices and narratives. The idea of 'lifestyle' extended beyond the various youth sub-cultures where they had first been consciously realised to encompass age groups both younger and older than themselves. As Gilleard and Higgs (2005) argue, the boundaries of the generational field that originally constituted youth culture have grown progressively looser, while subsequent attempts to recreate 'new' and 'distinct' youth cultures have imploded. What has emerged is a 'post-generational culture' whose origins in the youth culture of that period have been progressively expanded and diversified over the lifecourse. As the market continued to foster consumer segmentation (thus maintaining its centrality as the dominant source of social differentiation), the idea of 'youthfulness' has been extended across the lifecourse. At the same time, the social stratification of time has been fragmented into ever-smaller micro-generational moments. Years replace decades as potential 'generational units', rendering periods in history and stages of life less solid points of reference from which to base a mass culture.

Equally important is the fact that as each successive cohort is socialised into the practices and narratives of recreational consumption, the lifecourse divisions established by a classical modernity become more permeable. All sections of the population have gained entry to a common post-generational habitus, sharing similar consumerist preoccupations with food and diet, fitness and health, lifestyle and leisure. Such habitus encourage people of differing ages to identify themselves as citizen consumers embedded within an all-enveloping mass culture of consumption. Just as the media helped create code and communicate the youth culture of the 1960s, so the media and the market continue to play the key role in sustaining it in the 21st century as the era of the baby boomers.

The ageing of youth culture or the maturing of consumer society?

What implications does this analysis have for the study of the social and cultural determinants of later life? While youth may possess universal qualities, youth culture is much more contingent. During the 1950s and 1960s in America and in Europe, a largely novel phenomenon emerged: the universal valuing of the autonomous working-class teen. In America, this image seemed to subvert the ideals of an aspiring middle-class consumer citizen, threatening to break the bond between earning the right to leisure by earning a decent living. In Europe, the transformation of the working-class teenager took a little longer to be established. But when it finally came, in the 1960s, it heralded the end of an historic working-class culture that, in different ways and in different countries, had valorised the working man as honest breadwinner, and his counterpart, the industrious working class matriarch, as the force that held the family together. The generational break between the 'habitus' of working class youth and those of their parents was one of the central features of the 1960s' cultural revolution.

Youth culture and mass consumer society share a common origin. But age itself was not the fundamental divide that it was claimed to be. The democratisation of the lifecourse had begun long before, when, in 1948, *Time* magazine announced that the US population had increased by 2,800,000 more 'consumers' (Hine, 2000, p 250). Working through the logic of a mass consumer society takes time. The universal youth culture that emerged in the 1950s was a phenomenon created by US advertisers at the same time as being a 'counter-cultural' reaction to the materialism of those who cut their teeth during the Depression (Hine, 2000, pp 237-8). By attributing to the 'older' generation the fossilised distinctions between 'popular' and 'high' culture, it was possible to agitate for a cultural revolution that pitted not working-class interests against middle-class interests, but the universal desire of youth against the particularities of age.

Once a victory of sorts had been established for youth culture as the universal vanguard of the new mass culture, scope for further cultural revolution became more limited. The vectors of that generational divide had been determined. All that subsequent birth cohorts could do was to follow and elaborate them. As those generational warriors grow older, taking with them much of the kudos and the more significant spoils of victory, further generational divisions are less easy to establish and, even when established, less easy to sustain. The question of what constituted youth culture is, in retrospect, difficult to answer. Does it define a particular historical period? Can or should it be distinguished from a 'youthful' period in the development of mass consumer society? As the material symbols of what was once portrayed as the 'youth revolution' fade and the individual icons of that period age, do they still function as the boundaries of a cultural field that was so age- (youth-) defined. Perhaps, those things that were once taken as representative of youth were really the symbols of a new stage in social relations, one that valorised authenticity over authority, consumption over production, novelty over familiarity, and partnership over parenthood. Defined not so much as an age group but as the product of a 'new' generational field, the third age is the continuing manifestation (or maturation) of what once was called youth culture. Rather than treating the third age as a particular 'lucky' cohort, it makes more sense to treat it as the cultural expression of a generational field that, born in classical modernity, has reached maturity in a period organised around different principles of consumption and identity.

Consumption and the generational field of ageing

In this way, the understanding of generations becomes crucial for understanding later life and its connection to consumption. We have represented the third age as a generational field whose origins lie in the youth culture of the 1950s and 1960s. Participants in post-war youth culture acquired habitus that have evolved and multiplied during the course of their lifetimes, and affected the lifestyles of cohorts born before and after them. Central to those habitus have been new styles and new approaches to consumption arising from mass culture (Kammen, 1999, p 179). What was novel about this new form of consumption was its capacity to generate 'lifestyles' that were differently fashioned from the 'styles of life' that were previously associated with particular classes occupying specific cultural niches in modern society. Consciousness of this transition and its underlying 'entelechy' was most often expressed by members of the 'radical' middle classes whose age placed them 'above' and 'to one side' of the real site of transition (Marwick, 1998, p 67). It was this group that spoke of youth's desire to break away from a society where 'you knew who people were from the way they spoke, you knew where they came from, the way they dressed, you knew what sort of jobs' (Gunn and Bell, 2002, p 115). While this mood of protest traversed many of the distinctions of class and crossed the boundaries of national communities, its true significance was its emergence within a growing mass culture that was capable of being extended to, expressed and acted on at every stage of life. Socialisation into the new lifestyles of consumption has permeated the lives not only of the participants of post-war youth culture, but also of those who have grown up since the watershed era of the 1960s.

The cultural space of the third age continues to be underpinned by the capacity to spend. As with its origins, so now as it is expressed in the lifestyles of 'modern maturity', this is not the 'conspicuous consumption' of the early 20th century described by Veblen (Veblen, 1953). Rather, it is consumption arising from the sense of agency and the search for distinction and pleasure that were first formed in the emerging sub-cultures of the 1960s. The expression of those aspirations forms the lifestyle habitus that define the third age. Two conditions were necessary for its emergence: first, an expansion in the number of people with discretionary spending power, and second, the creation of new sites of consumption, disembedded from the communal settings of the past. As 'self-service' became the dominant form of consumption – exemplified in the new supermarkets, the fashion boutiques, record shops and new-style department stores – individualisation and differentiation became key. Mass culture involved the rejection of older forms of popular culture, replacing them with increasingly segmented, crosscutting lifestyles that maintained difference from the past and distinction in the present.

Conclusion

As one commentator of the time argued, the 1950s and 1960s were as much a 'neophiliac' as a 'youth-oriented' culture (Brooker, 1970). A desire for what was 'now', what was new and different, was valued in and of itself. This was not so much as in earlier modernity because the new was a synonym for progress, but because it served to distance this 'new' generation from that of the 'old'. The desire to embrace what was new and reject what was old was felt at least as strongly by working-class youth as it was by the middle class. It focused on sources of horizontal differentiation, eliding 'youth' with 'freedom' and 'leisure'. In that sense, the origins of the third age lie in a cultural field that early on defined itself as resistance to the constrictions and limitations of 'old' ways and 'old' styles of living. Past habits of consumption constrain future opportunities. Those who grew up spending freely earlier in life are more likely to continue to spend freely later in life (Roberts, 2004). In the generational field of the first half of the 20th century, consumption as a site of agency was quite restricted, particularly for the majority of the working-class population. The differentiation that could be achieved within classes was considerably less than that between classes. Hence, class-based cultures and class-based styles of life formed the dominant sources of social differentiation. Further differentiation was restricted by the limited availability of goods and services, the constraints imposed by existing moral communities of taste, and the limited existence of discretionary spending. In the first decades of the 20th century, food alone consumed over half of all the costs of living, and for the working classes, 95% of family expenditure was devoted to purchasing the necessities of food, housing, fuel and clothing[3]. By contrast, in the early 21st century, only 18% of household expenditure is used to purchase 'leisure goods and services', while food accounts for 16% [4]. The post-war expansion of discretionary spending across much of the general population and its subsequent extension over much of the lifecourse has offered more people than ever access to the agency of 'lifestyle choices'. Individual differentiation has become the dominant aspect of contemporary societies and is as much a part of the everyday life of larger and larger numbers of older people as they bring their generational experiences into this stage of the lifecourse. In the next chapter, we turn to evidence of trends in participation of older people in consumer society.

Notes

[1] Mannheim refers to generational entelechy as a style specific to a generation and links this explicitly to the speed of social change: 'When as a result of an acceleration in the tempo of social and cultural transformation basic attitudes must change so quickly that the latent, continuous adaptation and modification of traditional patterns of experience, thought and expression is no longer possible, then the various new phases of experience are consolidated somewhere, forming a clearly distinguishable new impulse, and a new centre of configuration. We speak in such cases of the formation of a new generational style, or of a new generation entelechy' (Mannheim, 1952, p 308).

[2] For Bourdieu's elaboration of these terms, see Bourdieu and Wacquant (1996, pp 94-140), Bourdieu (1977, pp 72-95) and Wacquant (1989, pp 37-41).

[3] See Allen and Bewley (1935) *Family expenditure: A study of its variation*, Table, p 5, and Table A, first column, pp 32-3.

[4] Office for National Statistics (2002b), Table 1.2, p 17.

FOUR

Consumption and the changing nature of the household in later life

Introduction

Since antiquity, the household has been the basic organisational unit of western society. In ancient Greece, it was termed the *oikos* (from which is derived the term 'economy'), while in Rome, it was termed the *familia* (from which is derived the term 'family'). For the Greeks and Romans, as for most settled societies, the household was the central unit of production, consumption, enumeration and taxation. Besides being a site where goods and services were produced and consumed, the household was also the site of social reproduction where age, generation, gender and sexuality were enacted and personal identities formed and sustained. As times have changed, the nature of the household has changed, both in its size and in its composition, as well as its role in the economy. This chapter addresses aspects of continuity and change within the household during the second half of the 20th century, particularly as these changes have affected older people. Specifically, it examines the household as a unit of consumption and how this reflects on the lives and lifestyles of older adults.

Prior to the introduction of old-age pensions, the viability of maintaining an independent household for an older person was limited. It depended on some combination of accessible family support, an independent income, continuing wage labour and/or self-employment. In countries such as Britain that had a fairly comprehensive poor law system, some older people did manage to maintain a separate own household even when they could not work, through the provision of outdoor relief. The solution for surviving in their later life, for the majority of people, was to share a household with other, younger people. Failure meant institutionalisation and the poorhouse. In 1892, 21% of the population aged 65 and over in England and Wales received outdoor relief, while 8.3% (114,000 people) lived in the poorhouse (Nield, 1898).

As pensions replaced poor relief as a more reliable source of later life income, fewer people needed to labour on in later life. Pension income remained limited, however, and up until the Second World War the majority of old-age pensioners in Britain, as in most of Europe, lived with younger adults, usually their children. After the war, as regular retirement income became the norm, the numbers of older people able to live alone increased. Even so, during the 1940s and 1950s, the majority of people of pensionable age still lived with younger adults. In 1947, in Wolverhampton, half the people of pensionable age were living with their children and a further 10% with other relatives. Fifty-three percent of people of pensionable age in Oldham, 62% in York and 75% in mid-Rhondda (South Wales) were living with their children (Townsend, 1963, p 34). During the 1960s, further change took place. The numbers of pensioners living alone or with other pensioners grew and by the time the Family Expenditure Surveys used in this book were under way, pensioner-only households had become the dominant household model for people aged 60 and over (Gazeley, 2003, Table 6.11, p 174).

As we have seen in earlier chapters, during the second half of the 20th century an important transition took place in the conditions that structure later life. Consumption became more salient in how people lived and defined their lives. This transition to mass affluence has led to a concomitant shift in how people construe their life and their social identity, from one based on participation in the productive processes of society to one dominated by consumerist lifestyles (Ransome, 2005). How far the opportunities associated with mass consumption and mass communication can be realised depends on the resources people have at their command. While retirement and the 'empty nest' once constituted a major risk for social and economical marginalisation, current evidence suggests that active consumption characterises older households as much as it does younger households. This chapter considers how much changes in household structure have facilitated or held back the consumerist transformation of post-working life. Specifically, it examines the extent to which patterns of consumption in 'pensioner-only' households differs from that of people of pensionable age living in 'non-pensioner' households. The question we shall focus on is whether the majority of people in their sixties who live in pensioner-only households have been less active participants in mass consumer society compared with their age peers who have remained within multi-generational households.

The changing nature of late-life households in the Family Expenditure Surveys

The household files of the Family Expenditure Surveys (FESs) from 1968 to 1998 provide a glimpse into the changing nature of late-life households, a glimpse that can be tied in to patterns of household goods ownership and sources of expenditure. In this first section, we compare the changing situation of householders in their sixties and the proportion who are living with people of working age (16-59) or younger during this period. We concentrate on this particular age decade group because the FES household data files do not further distinguish age decade groups after the age of 70 (with the exception of those who are designated household heads). Hence the focus is very much on new cohorts of 'pensioners'. The data were selected from four separate year files of the FES of Great Britain[1] chosen to represent three 10-year intervals over the period 1968 to 1998. Details of the FES and methods used in analysing the surveys are provided in the Appendix.

For the purpose of the analysis presented in this chapter, however, households were divided on the basis of their age composition. We used a threefold grouping of 'children and young people' (0-15 yrs), 'adults of working age' (16-59) and adults aged 60-69 years of age (60+). Each household was the unit of analysis. We focused on those households that contained anyone aged 60-69 years, with information on household social status extracted from the information available on the consumption patterns associated with the head of household.

As Table 4.1 shows, there has been a trend towards continuing age segregation, for people in their sixties as well as, more markedly, for those aged over 70 years old. While over a quarter of people over 70 lived with people under 60 years of age in 1968, that figure had dropped to one in 10 by the end of the century; likewise, while over one third of the people in their sixties lived with people under 60 in 1968, that figure had dropped to a quarter by 2001.

How far has this age-group segregation affected patterns of household consumption? Are households with only people aged 60 and over less likely to engage in surplus consumption? We explored this question in a number of ways. First, we looked at patterns of household expenditure devoted to necessities. We used the same criteria as the English Longitudinal Study of Ageing (ELSA) study group, when examining age-associated indicators of household welfare, that is, the proportion of expenditure devoted to food, fuel and clothing (Banks and Leicester, 2006). Higher proportionate spends indicate proportionately lower expenditures on 'non-necessities' such as leisure, travel and personal goods and services. We next examined the proportionate spend on necessities for all those

Table 4.1: Analysis of household composition for people aged 60-69 and 70+, 1968-98

Year	No. of households surveyed	No. of households with people aged 60-69 years old	No. of people aged 60-69 years old	No. of people aged 60-69 years old, living with 16- to 59-year-olds and/or under-16-year-olds	No. of people aged 70 years and over	No. of people aged 70 years and over, living with 16- to 59-year-olds and/or under-16-year olds
1968	7,183	1,560	2,070	695 (33.6%)	1,407	379 (26.9%)
1973	7,124	1,632	2,175	712 (32.7%)	1,531	344 (22.5%)
1978	7,001	1,467	1,931	561 (29.1%)	1,559	258 (16.5%)
1983	6,973	1,433	1,900	494 (26.0%)	1,632	231 (14.2%)
1988	7,265	1,406	1,879	555 (29.5%)	1,767	214 (12.1%)
1993	6,979	1,227	1,616	391 (24.2%)	1,762	188 (10.7%)
1998	6,409	1,067	1,386	380 (27.4%)	1,540	159 (10.3%)
2001	6,637	1,186	1,543	401 (25.9%)	1,668	163 (9.8%)

Source: FES

households that contained someone aged 60-69 years, divided into those living with and those not living with someone aged under 60 years of age. The data are presented in Figure 4.1. While there was a significantly greater expenditure on household necessities by households made up of people only aged 60 and over compared with households with people both over and under age 60 from 1968 to 1993, after 1993 these differences were insignificant.

Figure 4.1: Households with people in their sixties: proportionate spend on necessities by presence/absence of others aged 59 or younger, 1968-2001

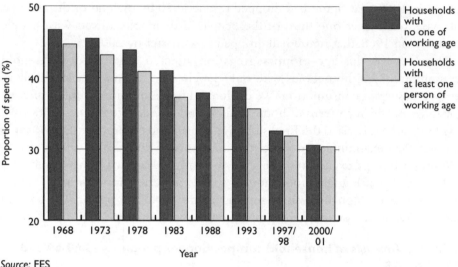

Source: FES

Applying an analysis of variance to the household expenditure data, there was a small but significant interaction between period and the absence or presence of people aged 59 or younger. The implication is that by the end of the 20th century, the presence or absence of adults of working age no longer influenced the household welfare of people in their sixties.

We made a further examination of the effect of sharing a household with people of working age (16-59 years old) on the household consumption of people in their sixties, by looking at household ownership of key consumer goods over this period. Because of the shifting nature of consumption, the goods that were recorded at each survey were quite limited. We have therefore confined our analysis to a basket of five consumer durables: TV, telephone, washing machine, fridge/fridge-freezer and car. The number of these goods owned by households with people in their sixties was computed for the period 1973 to 2001, with households categorised as before between those with people of working age (16-59 years old) and those without. As Figure 4.2 shows, a similar pattern of growing parity over time is

Figure 4.2: Ownership of key consumer durables in households with people in their sixties, by presence/absence of others aged 59 or younger, 1973-2001

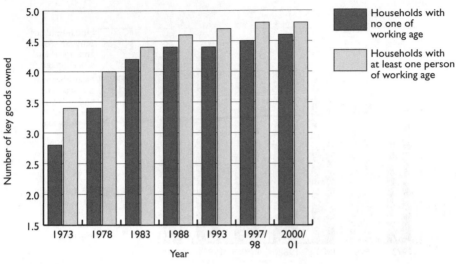

Source: FES

evident. Households that included people of working age as well as people in their sixties initially owned more key consumer durables than households made up only of people aged 60 and over during the 1970s, but by the 1980s there was evident catch-up, as most households possessed all five consumer durables. This changed little up to the end of the century.

Finally, we compared the position of households with people aged 70 and above living in them on the same index, with that of households with people in their sixties, each age group separated into those with and those without people of working age. The results are presented in Figure 4.3, where it can be seen that all households with people aged 60 and over shared a common trend towards increasing ownership of all five consumer durables, as well as a growing convergence in the ownership of consumer durables, irrespective of the presence or absence of people of working age in the household. Households with people in their sixties showed a higher level of ownership and a slightly greater convergence in ownership trends, compared with households with people in their seventies or older.

Conclusion

The FESs analysed in this chapter started when the post-war boom was well under way. The trends evident in our 30-year period capture the confluence in mass consumption that had begun well before, in the 1950s. For example, the total

Figure 4.3: Ownership of key consumer durables in households with people in their sixties, compared with households with people aged 70 and above, categorised by presence/absence of others aged 59 or younger, 1973-2001

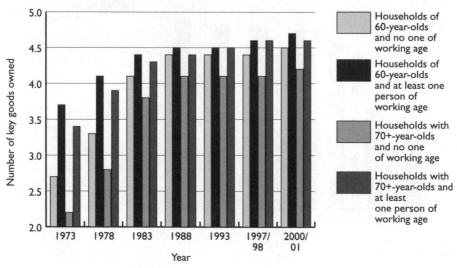

Source: FES

number of cars in Great Britain rose from 1.5 million at the end of the Second World War to 8.9 million by 1965, while the number of TV sets rose from none to almost 15 million (Bédarida, 1979, pp 256, 264). The analyses that we have presented here need to be set in that context. What they still manage to illustrate is the increased viability of pensioner households and their growing capacity to become sites of mass consumption, mirroring trends that had earlier characterised households containing adults of working age. Despite the slow but steady 'age segregation' of British households, throughout this 30-year period, consumer citizenship in later life has expanded with increasing convergence in patterns of consumption between households containing adults of working age as well as older people and households containing only older people.

Rather than view the multi-generational living of the first half of the 20th century as a sign of a cultural richness that we have since lost, we must recognise how much that pattern of shared households reflected the mass impoverishment of a society when the consumption of sugar and tobacco was considered a suitable indicator of surplus expenditure. The consequence of not living together could well have been living in the workhouse. This transformation has been illustrated in two ways. First, there has been a decline in the proportion of spending on the necessities of life (food, clothes and fuel). Spending on life's necessities declined at least as much, if not more, for households made up entirely of people aged 60 and over, as it did for households that also contained people of working age.

But the story of these 30 years is not just about declining hardship in later life. Household ownership of key consumer durables has also become more equivalised. The number of people of pensionable age who are in a position, alone or together, to access goods associated with the comfort and leisure of a post-scarcity society, irrespective of the presence of people of working age in the household, represents, in concrete form, a realisation of the choice, autonomy, self-expression and pleasure that helps define, as we have argued here and elsewhere, the cultural field of the third age. The next chapter takes this analysis further by examining trends in patterns of ownership of key goods in more detail by comparing retired households with employed and unemployed households.

Note

[1] The Office for National Statistics also conducts the Northern Ireland Family Expenditure Survey, which is very similar to the FES. However, these data were not included in our analyses.

FIVE

Later life in consumer society

Introduction

As we have seen in Chapters One and Two, the closing decades of the 20th century saw significant social changes in the nature of later life, some of which reflect the emergence of 'consumer societies' in the UK and elsewhere. The uneven nature of retirement, as well as the relative affluence of many retired people and the poverty of others, influence the experience and patterns of consumption in later life. Several key writers have pointed out how social identities are increasingly formed around processes of consumption rather than those of production and reproduction (Beck, 1991; Bauman, 1998; Zukin and Maguire, 2004). While research on the link between consumption and identity has been carried out on young or working-age groups (Hebdidge, 1979; Nixon, 1996), gerontological researchers have often presumed that older people are outside the cultural dynamics of consumption or implicitly assumed that such dynamics play little part in the day-to-day lives of older people (Gilleard, 1996; Gilleard and Higgs, 2000). However, as several commentators are aware (Dychtwald, 1999; Freedman, 1999; Metz and Underwood, 2005), the cohorts of people retiring today are those who pioneered the creation of the post-war consumer culture. The decades of the 1950s, 1960s and 1970s saw the emergence of new, youth-orientated consumer markets directed at cohort located sub-cultures. While the absolute numbers of people making up the 'baby-boomer' or 'baby-bulge' cohorts was certainly important, this was not the main reason for their significance. Young people during this period had money and they also had an increasing range of non-essential items to spend it on (Bocock, 1993). These new consumer opportunities went further than just providing outlets for fashion and conspicuous expenditure; they provided the basis for generational identities that continue to be played out decades later. The post-war cohorts both lived through the emergence of the 'affluent society' and participated in creating contemporary consumer society. The emphasis on choice in what they wore, as well as in the entertainment they consumed, and the goods they owned, provided the stimulus for a mass consumer culture that was different from what had gone before (Kammen, 1999).

The once young consumers of the post-war period have grown older, all the while retaining their propensities to be active players in a society where the pursuit of lifestyle and identity is as likely to emerge out of the commodities purchased as it is out of the ascribed identities of employment. This later-life consumption is not undifferentiated. As at earlier points in the lifecourse, it is necessary to see such activities as multi-layered phenomena; consumers are differentiated not only in terms of their cohort and generation but also in terms of their social location, income and wealth. Their collective and individual histories frame their current consumption choices and influence future ones. Those born at earlier times had less opportunity to participate in the formation of consumer society and were less engaged with it (Kramper, 2000). Studies on generational patterns of consumption in modern society have tended to neglect the changing cultural context of consumption patterns of older people (Gunter, 1998). Crucial to understanding ageing today therefore is to understand the differences between and within generations (Arber and Attias-Donfut, 1999).

In this chapter, we describe the nature of older people's participation in consumer society over the past four decades. We examine patterns of consumption at different time points between the 1960s and the end of the 20th century. By comparing trends in household ownership of key consumer durable goods among heads of households by labour market status, we are able to examine the relative rates of uptake of these goods among retired households. We do this first in relation to goods that penetrated mass consumer markets at an early point in the time period – telephones, television sets and washing machines – sometimes referred to as standardised consumer durables. Second, we repeat the analysis in relation to the adoption of newer commodities – video cassette recorders (VCRs), microwave ovens and personal computers (PCs) – sometimes referred to as novel consumer durables. We also consider ownership of dishwashers and cars to illustrate continuing differences between retired and other households. The data provide some evidence of older people's increasing (but possibly uneven) engagement with consumer society through ownership of key goods. This chapter and the following two chapters are based on a secondary analysis of the Family Expenditure Survey (FES) data. Full details of our methodology are provided in the Appendix. In this chapter, however, the aim is to illustrate the increasing engagement of older households with consumer society by drawing comparisons between retired and working households. Chapter Six examines the uneven nature of these trends.

Trends in ownership among older households

We begin by looking at trends in ownership of household goods among older households. As Figure 5.1 shows, ownership of telephones, TVs and fridges/fridge-freezers reached saturation by the end of the period studied.

Rates of ownership of washing machines were close to 90% by the end of the century, while ownership of microwaves and VCRs increased rapidly following their later emergence. The rate of take-up of goods among older households therefore varied according to the type of goods involved, with some showing a steady long-term rise and other showing steeper trajectories. Goods such as PCs and dishwashers show an increase in ownership, but again emerged later and

Figure 5.1: Trends in ownership of household goods, 1968-2001

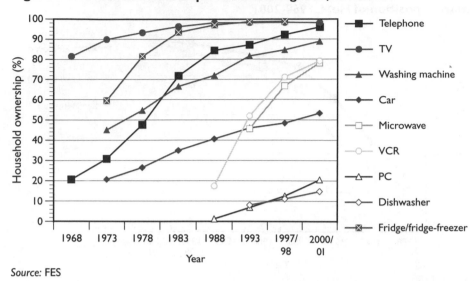

Source: FES

remain relatively low in terms of ownership levels. Car ownership increased from a low of 20% in the early 1970s to over 50% at the end of the century.

Comparing older and younger households

Pausing to focus on older households over the last 30 years of the 20th century, there is evidence of a general picture of progressive take-up of key consumer goods with some variation according to the type of goods examined. But how does this compare with younger and working households? One way of doing this is to compare rates of ownership according to the labour market status of the household. To do this, we utilise a three-way comparison between employed, retired and unemployed households.

Figure 5.2 compares the proportions of households that owned a telephone for the different labour market position of the head of household (HoH) from 1968 to 2001. What is immediately striking about these figures are the low percentages in the 1960s of households that owned a telephone regardless of the labour market position of the HoH. In 1968, about one third of households where the HoH was in employment owned a telephone, compared with about a quarter of those who were retired and a fifth of those who were unemployed. Over the period, this increased for all groups and by 2001, almost 100% of households headed by an employed HoH or a retired HoH owned a telephone, while just over 90% of households headed by an unemployed HoH had one.

Figure 5.3 shows that although there were high levels of TV ownership even in 1968 for all three groups, there were still disparities, with 93% of households

Figure 5.2: Percentage of households owning a telephone, by labour market position of HoH, 1968-2001

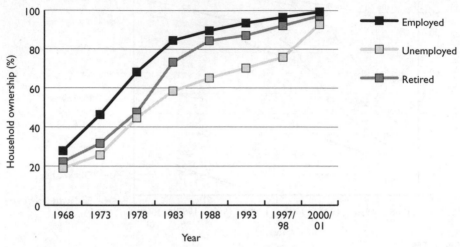

Source: FES

Figure 5.3: Percentage of households owning a television, by labour market position of HoH, 1968-2001

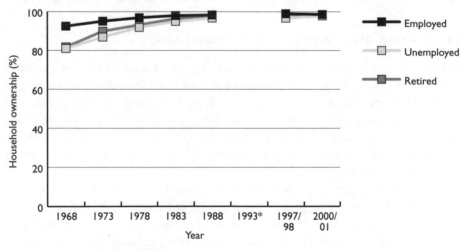

Note: * Data not available for 1993.
Source: FES

with an employed HoH owning a TV compared with 81% of households with a retired HoH. Again by 2001, however, almost all households, whether employed, retired or unemployed, owned a TV set.

Figure 5.4 shows the proportion of households that owned a washing machine for the different labour market position of the HoH from 1973 to 2001. Although

Figure 5.4: Percentage of households owning a washing machine, by labour market position of HoH, 1973-2001

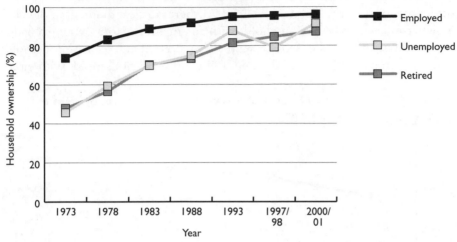

Source: FES

the absolute levels of ownership rise for all groups, there are differences across the three groups at each year, with those in households with an employed HoH with the highest levels of ownership – 74% in 1973, rising to 96% in 2001. The retired and unemployed lag behind the employed in ownership of washing machines, but closely match each other, except for some minor variations, throughout the

Figure 5.5: Percentage of households owning a fridge/fridge-freezer, by labour market position of HoH, 1973-97

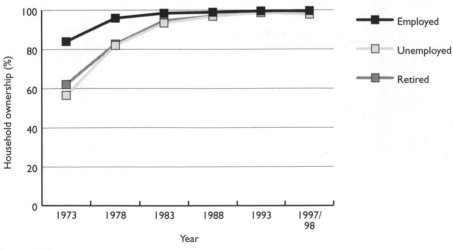

Source: FES

period. High levels of ownership are achieved in all HoH types by the end of the century.

The trend in household ownership of fridges/fridge-freezers shows much clearer patterns of convergence (Figure 5.5). In 1973, there is a clear gradient in the rates of ownership, with 84% of households with an employed HoH owning a fridge compared with 62% of households with a retired HoH and 57% of households with an unemployed HoH. By the mid-1980s, however, households with either

Figure 5.6: Percentage of households owning a microwave, by labour market position of HoH, 1993-2001

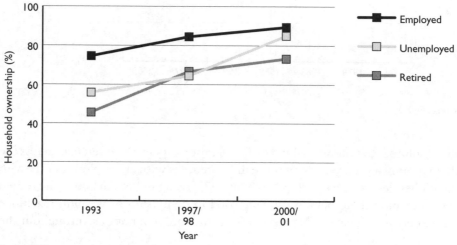

Source: FES

Figure 5.7: Percentage of households owning a VCR, by labour market position of HoH, 1993-2001

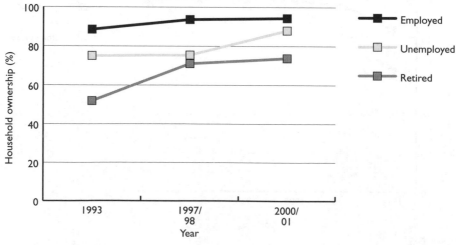

Source: FES

Figure 5.8: Percentage of households owning a PC, by labour market position of HoH, 1988-2001

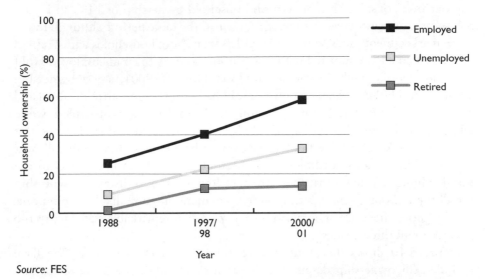

Source: FES

Figure 5.9: Percentage of households owning a dishwasher, by labour market position of HoH, 1993-2001

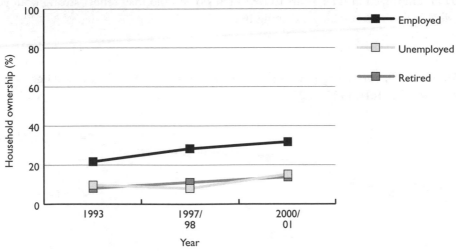

Source: FES

a retired or unemployed HoH have caught up, with saturation being achieved by the early 1990s.

Figures 5.6 to 5.9 show the results for the most contemporary goods we have been able to measure. The data for household ownership of microwave ovens and for VCRs show similar patterns, albeit over shorter time frames. In 1993, there are clear inequalities in ownership. Households with a retired HoH reported lower levels of ownership than either households with an employed HoH or an unemployed HoH. While this inequality persists across 1997 and 2001 surveys, this gap narrows considerably. The data on household ownership of a PC, in Figure 5.8, shows some evidence of convergence across the same period, although much more marked inequalities persist. In 1993, less than 2% of households with a retired HoH owned a PC compared with 9% of households with an unemployed HoH and a quarter of households with an employed HoH. By 2001, rates of ownership among households with an employed HoH had slightly more than doubled and rates among households with an unemployed HoH had almost tripled, while rates among households with a retired HoH had increased tenfold. Despite this dramatic uptake of new technology by retired households, they were still over 75% less likely than households with an employed HoH to have a PC in the house. Figure 5.9 shows that there are very low levels of dishwasher ownership for all three groups, although those in employment are more likely to own one. Furthermore, the levels of ownership have remained remarkably static across the period for all three groups.

Figure 5.10 shows the results for household ownership of a car. We have included car ownership, despite the fact that one could question its status as a household good. Here the pattern is different than that already presented for the other goods. Although there is a clear rise in the absolute levels of ownership for all groups, the rate of convergence between retired households and those headed by an employed HoH appears to be much slower and may reflect strong cohort effects relating to owning a driving licence.

Figure 5.10: Percentage of households owning a car, by labour market position of HoH, 1973-2001

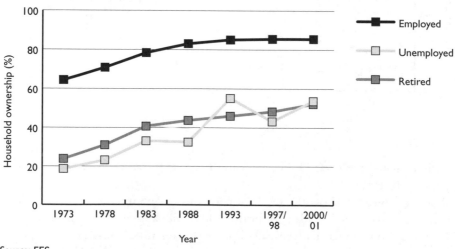

Source: FES

Later life and the emergence of consumer society

Our argument in this book is that later life in Britain has changed dramatically since the 1960s. Of primary importance to our argument is the emergence and centrality of a consumer society in Britain. Such a society can only be said to exist if there is widespread ownership of consumer durables and the adoption of new types of consumer goods by large sectors of society. The data presented here demonstrate that there has been a general growth in the ownership of household goods in Britain since the 1960s and that this growth has also kept pace with the development of new technologies and goods. These goods range from fridges and microwave ovens on the one hand to VCRs and PCs on the other. Within such ownership, differentiation does occur. However, unlike earlier examples of consumption where ownership was confined to particular groups or strata, the modern mass markets have maximised penetration for the population as a whole. Non-ownership of many goods such as cars and TV can lead to forms of social exclusion. Car ownership, which was a minority experience in the 1960s, has, like telephone and TV ownership, crossed a boundary from being a luxury consumer good to an essential household item and thus become normative. Similarly, developments within consumer markets led to new products and models becoming available and ownership becoming more diffuse. By setting up expectations, such market diffusion engages all sections of the population in consumer practices whether or not they actually own particular goods.

Our data demonstrate not only that there has been markedly increased ownership of certain goods, but also that this has occurred for working, retired and unemployed households. These results are unsurprising for the employed households, given the continued rise in both incomes and standards of living across this period (Benson, 1994; Self and Zealey, 2007). However, contrary to accounts focusing on poverty in later life, the data demonstrate that, at the beginning of the 21st century, retired households are increasingly similar in their patterns of ownership of many household goods to the rest of the population.

The data also suggest that the early 1980s appear to be a key transitional point for the convergence of ownership patterns between these groups. However, there are several types of goods identifiable in the FES that do not follow this pattern, including dishwashers, tumble dryers and microwave ovens. This difference is significant because it allows us to speculate on the factors that may be inferred from the ownership or non-ownership of certain goods. For example, factors such as the size of the average kitchen may limit the take up of dishwashers and the same may be true for tumble dryers (Freeman, 2004). An additional factor may be household composition; the presence of young children may necessitate more regular washing and drying than would be the case for other households. Likewise, ownership of microwave ovens exhibits a trend that sees unemployed households having greater ownership than retired ones. This may in part be due to the fact that such ovens often offer a cheaper option for cooking than conventional cookers. It may also reflect the fact that, like the employed households, such unemployed households are younger and microwaves a relatively recent innovation and thus more likely to be seen as normative. It is important to remember that this is a preliminary analysis based on broad household categories and that further differentiation within these broad groups is necessary to elaborate these patterns.

It is also important to be aware of the limitations of the data available in the FES. A potentially serious consideration is that these data only relate to whether the good is or is not present in the household. Thus we have no information on the quality or cost of the product, its (symbolic) meaning for the consumer or how it is used, or by whom it is used, in the household. Consequently, our interpretations can only be based on the facts of ownership. It is conceivable that retirees are not purchasing new goods but buying older or even second-hand versions of these consumer products. If this were the case, it would suggest that older people are less fully engaged in consumer culture and are operating with a more utilitarian approach to these household items. Also, as Vincent (1999) points out, the accumulation of different goods over the course of years may create problems of compatibility that affect ownership patterns.

While we cannot discount these possibilities or directly test them with these data, the uptake of microwave ovens, VCRs and to some extent PCs points to retired households engaging with goods that have a cultural significance. Ownership of these goods represents engagement not only with new forms of consumer-orientated technology, but also, in the case of VCRs and PCs, with entertainment. While it is possible that these goods are not used to their full potential – the PC may be used solely as a typewriter in older households, for example – these products do allow access to a greater level of engagement with popular culture. This in turn suggests that retired households are not simply satisfied with watching programmes on TV but want to be able to access the latest films and, by extension, participate in popular culture to the same extent as the rest of the population. Obviously, in order to do this, they require the appropriate technology – the VCR (and now the DVD player). If retired people simply operated with a utilitarian approach to (audio-visual) entertainment and simply wanted to watch programmes, there would be no reason to purchase VCRs, as TVs continue to show programmes.

Entertainment is increasingly a crucial aspect of consumer culture and it is not surprising that levels of ownership show such rapid rises. These increases, however, also need to be situated within the markets in which they operate. VCRs are rapidly being superseded by DVD players. In order to keep up with market-dominant entertainment formats, it is now necessary to have both. Future data may show a decline in VCR ownership but a rapid increase in DVD players or even by their replacement, hard drive digital recorders. In a similar fashion, vinyl records have been replaced by CDs, which are now being made obsolete by MP3 systems. Each innovation requires new purchases in order to keep pace with the market and to be able to participate in contemporary society. Alongside PC ownership, the ownership of these key goods shows how engaged in a consumer culture retired people are. Unlike telephones and TVs, there is no benefit in passive ownership and no equivalent of the low-user telephone tariff. A further limitation could be that the acquisition of goods is more of a result of younger family members bringing them into a household with older people living in it rather than older people owning these goods themselves. Nevertheless, it is significant that the percentages of multi-generational households headed by someone who is over state retirement age for the sample declines from just under 20% in 1968 to just over 10% in 2001, with the figures being lower for female-headed households.

Conclusion

The data we have presented here demonstrate that there is evidence for the argument that in relation to ownership of key consumer goods retired households are becoming much more similar to working households. We can see that over time the ownership of key consumer items by different sections of the population converges. There has been a gradual increase in car ownership by working, unemployed and retired households and an almost total saturation of the ownership of televisions and telephones. This pattern may go hand in hand with the growing affluence experienced by most sections of the population, but particularly by large proportions of those in retirement or who have moved into retirement since the early 1980s. Even among those households that are recorded as having an unemployed HoH, we see a pattern of convergence that may in part reflect the episodic nature of most unemployment (except for a period during the 1980s, where, interestingly, car ownership is higher among the retired than the unemployed). This should not be surprising because increasing ownership of such goods goes with prosperity in countries where real incomes have risen (ONS, 2002a). What appears to be occurring is that ownership of key goods is spreading out across the whole population. Ownership of refrigerators shows a pattern consistent with increasing ubiquity. However, even with this everyday object, we can see how both necessity and culture interact. The ownership of separate fridges and freezers and their separate counting could reflect a social division that made the freezer a desirable consumer item but did not last long enough in popular consciousness for it to avoid being subsumed into the category fridge-freezer. In a similar fashion, ownership of washing machines has become normative in the majority of households, but not the ownership of tumble dryers.

These patterns of convergence in what could be termed essential as well as novel consumer durables suggest that over the past few decades the differences between the consumption patterns of the working and retired populations have diminished. This is not to say that inequalities do not persist (as we will see in Chapter Six), but the idea common in the mid-20th century that later life was dominated by poverty and exclusion from society no longer holds. If we link up these data of ownership with the more theoretical concerns of generation, we can postulate that over the period in question, there has been a general trend of growing engagement with consumer society. While such broad stroke patterns of ownership cannot explicitly tell us about the cultural dynamics being experienced by successive cohorts of retired people, they can show that, as British society becomes more concerned with consumption, so do older people. Once again, this is not surprising because, as we have argued earlier, these are the same people who brought into existence many of the features of consumer society. The ownership of key goods relating to entertainment could be seen as an aspect of this as cohorts of post-war consumers take their engagement with popular culture into retirement with them. The direction of engagement with consumer society by older people is towards greater involvement, even if it seems that older people are not seen as primary markets by advertisers or that the representation of later life is ageist.

Our intention in this chapter has been to show how even at its simplest level – the ownership of goods – the retired population is not only present in consumer society but has also become very similar to the rest of the population in its engagement with it. Further work is needed on showing the inter-relationship between different cohorts, gender, consumption and retirement in order to deepen our understanding of how later life has been transformed by the generational habitus of the first generations of the consumer society. It is to these more detailed questions that we turn in the following chapters.

SIX

Income, expenditure and inequalities in later life

Introduction

In Chapter One we noted that the UK experienced considerable income growth from the 1960s onwards despite prolonged periods of economic crisis and high unemployment (Atkinson, 2000). Many older people benefited from these increases in income so that the economic position of older people has improved markedly over the past few decades in Britain as it has in most of the advanced industrialised world (Disney and Whitehouse, 2001; Casey and Yamada, 2002). This improvement creates winners and losers, with retirement age couples doing considerably better than single pensioners and women, particularly women who become widows, benefiting less (DWP, 2007). The overall rise in living standards was accompanied by growing inequalities in income from the 1960s onwards, particularly during the period between 1979 and 1997. The growth in income inequality among the working age population in Britain during the 1980s was exceptionally high (Atkinson, 1999) and rising income inequality continued through to the end of the century, but changes since 2000 are less clear (Dorling et al, 2007). Income mobility among the retired population increased with marked reductions in poverty rates, and the overall variability in pensioner incomes increased rather less than within the working age population during these last two decades (Förster, 2000; Brown and Prus, 2006). Zaidi and colleagues (2005) account for the decline in the incidence of poverty among the elderly by referring to the fact that later (younger) cohorts were more likely to have had occupational pensions. Furthermore, their findings show that 'as measured by the Gini coefficient, income inequality has increased amongst older people in Great Britain' (Zaidi et al, 2005, p 551). Thus, while there has been a marked growth in real net pensioner income since the early 1980s and a fall in the number of pensioners below the poverty line (Hills and Stewart 2005), there remain substantial inequalities among the retirement age population (Hills, 2004; ONS/DWP, 2005). To quote Hills:

> ... an important change of the last twenty years has been the emergence of a group of relatively high-income pensioners with significant incomes from occupational pensions. This has led to a pattern of income polarization *within* the pensioner population. (Hills, 2004, p 89, emphasis in original)

With respect to older people, studies of inequality (either of income, wealth or expenditure) have been dominated by studies of poverty levels, highlighting the fact that large numbers of older people still live on low incomes (Bardasi et al, 2002; Hills, 2004). However, studies based on the Pensioner Income Series and longitudinal analyses of the British Household Panel Survey have begun to address broader questions – of income distribution, income inequality and income mobility (Disney and Whitehouse, 2001; Zaidi and De Vos, 2002; Zaidi et al, 2005). For example, differences in economic advantage between couples of pensionable age and single persons of pensionable age have grown since the mid 1980s (DWP, 2007, Figure 4.6, p 58).

Wealth and income are different concepts and differences in one do not necessarily mirror differences in the other, particularly among older age groups. Some 'aged' households are income poor but wealth rich (Dorling et al, 2007). One recent estimate indicates that a fifth of income-poor pensioners hold housing equity in excess of £100,000 (Dixon and Margo, 2006). Some scholars suggest that, as incomes become more mobile and subject to short-term volatility, expenditure may prove a better measure of household welfare as it measures 'permanent income', although more research is needed in this area (Blundell and Preston, 1998). Patterns of inequality in household expenditure may be somewhat different than those for income. Using the Gini coefficient (Gastwirth, 1972) for expenditure in Britain between 1974 and 2000, Goodman and Oldfield (2004) show that inequality fell in the early 1970s and then grew rapidly, reaching a peak in 1990 and falling back slightly towards the end of the 20th century. Inequality in expenditure increased to a lesser extent than income inequality over the period so that while inequality in expenditure declined after 1990, in terms of income, Britain is more unequal than at any time over the past 40 years.

In the UK, research has shown how poverty in old age is gendered (Ginn, 2001). This has been driven by differential access to occupational pensions as a result of differences in labour force participation rates, widowhood and differences in household circumstances (Even and Macpherson, 1990; Dahl et al, 2003). These differences have been persistent over time, although the nature and the magnitude of differences have changed as men's and women's work histories become more similar. Differences among older men and women may reflect differences in marital status and living arrangements rather than gender differences. Indeed, there is evidence to suggest that this is the case with respect to service utilisation, provision of informal care and participation in social networks (Del Bono et al, 2007).

With respect to health inequalities, research has produced ambiguous results, with some evidence of a narrowing in inequalities, some evidence of inequalities widening and some research suggesting that the direction of effect is dependent on the measure used and adjustments for the length of time since exiting the labour market (Hyde and Jones, 2007). Some studies have demonstrated a convergence in the health of those from different socio-economic positions in older age (Fox and Goldblatt, 1982; Townsend et al, 1988; Arber and Ginn 1993; Arber and

Lahelma, 1993). This is commonly explained as the result of mortality selection or survivor effects. Data from the UK suggests that differential survivorship within old age may have lessened as life expectancy seems to be growing more equal for people from manual and non-manual occupational backgrounds (ONS, 2007b). However, socio-economic inequalities persist (Marmot and Shipley, 1996; Donkin et al, 2002) and inequalities in morbidity certainly continue into later life (Parker et al, 1994; Rahkonen and Takala, 1998; Grundy and Glaser, 2000; Breeze et al, 2001; Mayer et al, 2001; Grundy and Sloggett, 2003).

Research in the health field has focused on two competing hypotheses to explain health inequality in later life. The accumulated deprivation thesis suggests that the level of health inequality related to socio-economic status (SES) in a cohort will increase as a cohort ages (Dannefer, 2003). In contrast, the 'divergence/convergence' hypothesis or 'age as leveller' hypothesis suggests a widening of inequalities up to early old age and a decrease in inequalities thereafter. The age as leveller hypothesis focuses on the link between educational advantage and inequality (Beckett, 2000). The accumulated disadvantage hypothesis emphasises the joint effect on inequality levels of long-term disadvantage on morbidity in old age for lower SES groups and a compression of morbidity at the end of life for higher SES groups. The divergence/convergence thesis, on the other hand, argues that the impact of cumulative effects on inequality is greater in middle age.

In old age, the impact of survivor effects and beneficial and protective effects of welfare policies should mean that health differences are less acute. Evidence from Canada based on the relationship between SES and health supports the accumulated disadvantage hypothesis (Prus, 2007). In contrast, analysis of retrospective and prospective data on US individuals suggests that at the group level there is a divergence/convergence effect in the relationship between education and health, while at the individual level there is a strong effect of cumulative disadvantage (Dupre, 2007). Another US study based on retrospective data looking at the effects of financial strain over the lifecourse found that persistent economic hardship had a significant effect on health outcomes in later life, while the effects of episodic hardship could be attenuated if no further hardship was endured over the lifecourse (Kahn and Pearlin, 2006). While these studies provide valuable insights into the relationship between lifecourse effects and health status in later life, they are not able to adequately control for cohort and period effects in their models. This could be due to the fact that, unlike in the past, those from lower socio-economic positions are surviving into older age, thus carrying their increased likelihood of poorer health beyond retirement. In this sense, later life, or at least the health profiles of those in later life, is coming to resemble more closely working age life.

The evidence for the heterogeneity of present cohorts of older people, along a number of dimensions, is persuasive. However, it remains to be seen how these differences are related to inequalities in consumption and expenditure. In the following sections, we examine the nature of inequalities in expenditure and ownership of household goods among older households from 1968 to 2001. Using data from the Family Expenditure Survey (FES), we consider trends in ownership and consumption in relation to levels of household income, gender, marital status, household structure, state pension, housing tenure and cohort of head of household. In doing so we address the extent to which trends in inequality are reflected in older households' engagement with consumer society and the social patterning this takes.

Trends in consumption by the income position of the head of household

In order to look at differences among the retired population, the data analysed here relates to trends in expenditure by retired households. Households were stratified according to equivalised income quintiles. We used the McClements Scale (Before Housing Costs) (McClements, 1977), as this is currently the most commonly used by the Office for National Statistics (ONS), which conducts the FES (Dunn and Gibbins, 2006). Figure 6.1 shows ownership of a household telephone by equivalised household income quintile between 1968 and 2001. The telephone is an important means of engaging in consumer society and telephone ownership has been associated with quality of life in later life (Barnes et al, 2006). Rates of telephone ownership for all but those in the highest income quintile were low in 1968. For the sample as a whole, only around 20% of retired households owned a telephone, showing clear income inequalities in ownership. In 1968,

Figure 6.1: Percentage of households owning a telephone, by equivalised household income quintile, 1968-2001

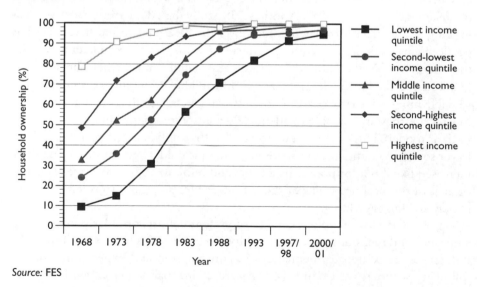

Source: FES

only around 10% of retired households in the lowest income quintile owned a telephone, compared with close to 80% in the highest income quintile. Although inequalities persist throughout the period, there is evidence that they become less stark. For example, by 1988, 70% of those in the lowest income quintile had a telephone, compared with almost 100% in the top two income quintiles. By 2000/01, these inequalities had all but disappeared and rates of telephone ownership had reached almost 100% for all income groups.

Telephones are an example where availability expanded and costs fell rapidly from the mid-1980s onwards, with subsequent saturation across all income groups of older households. If we move to a more recent technological development entering mass consumer markets, such as personal computers (PCs), we find a very different picture. Figure 6.2 shows rates of PC ownership by income quintile. In 1988, the first year for which the FES had data on PC ownership, rates are low (close to zero) for all income groups. By the 1990s, there is increasing differentiation between the top three income groups and the bottom two groups. In 1997/98, rates of PC ownership among those in the lowest income quintiles are still close to zero, while among those in the top three income groups, rates range from around 20-30%. By 2000/01, this differentiation is even more evident, with almost 50% of those in the top two income quintiles, while rates among those in the bottom three groups had not changed much from 1997/98.

As we have seen in Chapter One, over the last quarter of the 20th century there was a dramatic fall in the share of household expenditure on food, clothing and fuel and a sharp rise in spending on motor vehicles, holidays, private transport

Figure 6.2: Percentage of households owning a PC, by equivalised household income quintile, 1988-2001

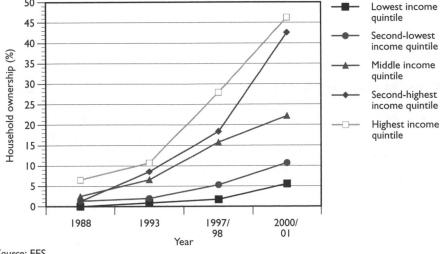

Source: FES

and eating out (Blow et al, 2004). However, there is evidence that not all groups of older people have shared equally in these trends. Data from the Consumer Expenditure Survey in the US show that those in the lower income groups spent a higher proportion of their income on food in 2005-06 (www.bls.gov). Figure 6.3 shows the proportion of total expenditure that is spent on food in older households. As expected, there is a clear downward pattern for all income groups. However, inequalities between the income groups are evident, with those in the lowest income groups spending a greater proportion of their income on food than those in the higher income groups. These inequalities remain fairly consistent across the period.

Figure 6.3: Expenditure on food as a percentage of total expenditure, by equivalised household income quintile, 1968-2001

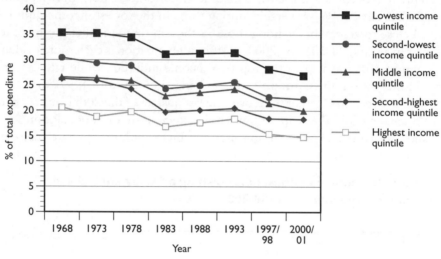

Source: FES

Trends in consumption by the sex of the head of household

We have noted previously that the general rise in incomes of older households has been uneven. Older women, largely because of their employment patterns, labour market inequity and their involvement in a variety of caring activities, are especially vulnerable to the experience of poverty and low income in old age (Ginn, 2001). These differences have been persistent over time, although the nature and the magnitude of difference have changed as men's and women's work histories have become more similar. Although the 'feminisation' of poverty in later life is strongly evident across Europe, this should not blind us to the differential impact of factors such as class and ethnicity on women's income levels in later life and indeed the presence of variations in income and pension levels between different cohorts of women (Ginn et al, 2002; Warren, 2006). If we look at ownership and expenditure by sex of head of household, it becomes apparent that there are some areas of expenditure where there is convergence and others where important inequalities remain. Beginning with TV ownership, Figure 6.4 shows ownership of a TV for older households by the sex of the head of household.

Figure 6.4: Percentage of households owning a TV, by sex of HoH, 1968-2001

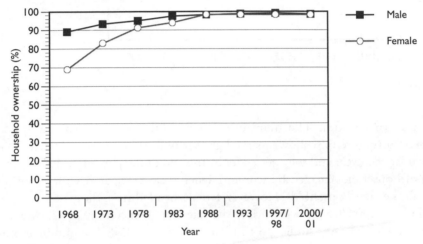

Source: FES

Although overall rates of TV ownership are high in 1968 compared with telephone ownership, there is a clear difference in the rates of ownership between those households headed by a man and those headed by a woman. The figure shows that in 1968 only around 70% of female-headed households had a TV compared with nearly 90% of male-headed households. However, these rates quickly converge and by 1988 almost 100% of all households had a TV. A car, like a TV, is a major consumption item. Cars have become a major focus of expenditure and a potent symbol of consumer society. Indeed, car ownership is routinely used as a measure of social status in its own right and has been shown to be associated with better health among older populations (Arber, 1991). However, the car is not only a consumer good, but is also a key factor in enabling participation in consumer culture. With the growth of 'out-of-town' shopping and the attendant decline of the high street, the ability to consume is increasingly reliant on the ability to travel. Thus, any differences in car ownership not only represent possible inequalities in consumption among retired households but also threaten to further exacerbate these divisions because of inequalities of access to a key facilitator

Figure 6.5: Ownership of a car by sex of HoH, 1973-2001

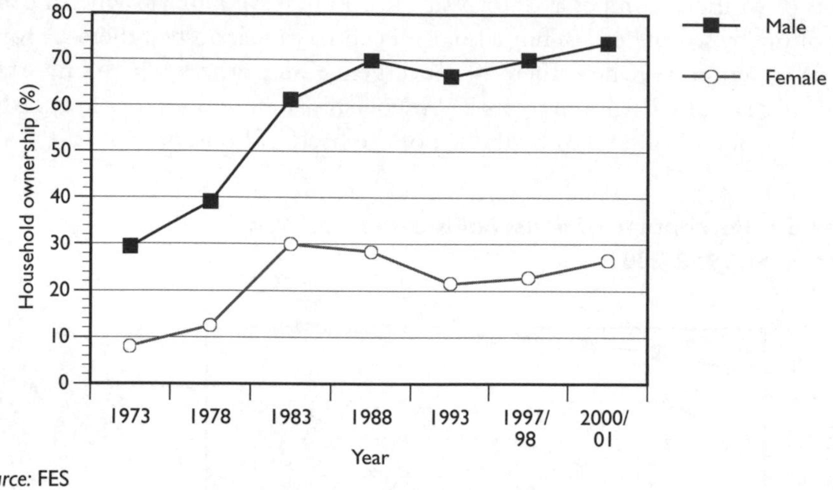

Source: FES

of social participation. The trend in car ownership by the sex of the head of household (Figure 6.5) shows marked gender differences. Here, inequalities are evident at each year and they get wider by the end of the period. In 1973, around 10% of households headed by women owned a car compared with about 30% of male-headed households. However, female-headed households only achieve this rate by 2000/01, by which time the rates for men have reached over 70%. These results are very similar to those found in the ONS Longitudinal Study (Breeze et al, 1999).

Trends in consumption by the marital status of the head of household

The discussion of trends in household composition in Chapter Four showed that between 1971 and 2006, the number of households in Britain increased by 30%, with the average household size falling over the same period from 2.9 to 2.4 people. In the UK, there was a considerable increase in one-person households over the last quarter of the 20th century. This increase is related to a pronounced rise in the number of widows and widowers and divorcees living alone. Between 1961 and 2001, there was a doubling in the proportion of people of pensionable age living alone. This has consequences for income and expenditure patterns in later life. For example, using Luxembourg Income Study data for nine countries in the Organisation for Economic Co-operation and Development, Casey and Yamada (2003) demonstrated that widows experience a substantial loss of income in countries where private pensions predominate (Britain, Canada and the US). If we look at ownership levels among older households by marital status of head of households, again we find interesting patterns of convergence and persisting

Figure 6.6: Ownership of a washing machine, by marital status of HoH, 1973-2001

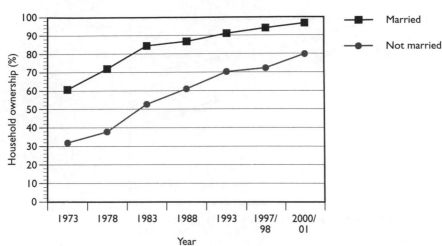

Source: FES

inequality. As Figure 6.6 shows, there are clear but narrowing inequalities in washing machine ownership between households where the head of household is married and those where they are unmarried. For example, in 1973, the first year for which we have data on washing machine ownership, just over 30% of unmarried households owned a washing machine compared with 60% of those where the head of household was married. However, by 2000/01, the proportions owning a washing machine had risen to 90% and 96%, respectively.

The pattern for VCR ownership is very different. In 1988, the rates of VCR ownership are relatively close, being around 10% in households with a non-married head of household and just under 30% in households with a married head of household. By 1997/98, although the rates had increased for both types of household, this gap had widened, with around half of unmarried households with a VCR compared with around 85% of married households. However, the gap narrows again slightly by 2001 due largely to the rates of ownership among married households levelling out.

Data on the proportion of total expenditure devoted to services for married and unmarried households show a potentially emerging inequality (Figure 6.7). Services include such things as postage, cinemas, laundry, domestic services and hairdressing. The range of goods included within the 'services' category and changes in the category over time makes these trends somewhat difficult to interpret. However, in 1968, both married and unmarried households devoted around 8% of their total expenditure on these services. Rates rose in unison by 1973 and began to fall thereafter. The rate of decline was steeper for married households, which by 2000/01 spent only 4%, compared with 8% for unmarried households at the end of the period.

Figure 6.7: Expenditure on services as a percentage of total expenditure, by marital status of HoH, 1968-2001

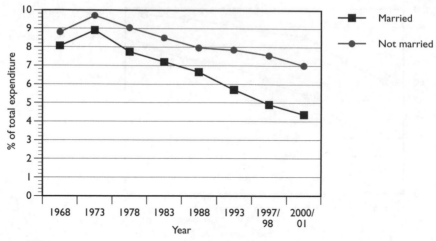

Source: FES

Trends in consumption by the household structure of the head of household

A potential explanation for the rise in consumption among older households could be that younger family members, who have either remained at home or returned to the parental home, are purchasing these goods rather than the older head of household. The rise of the 'adultescent', where offspring are leaving home at later and later ages, may distort the expenditure patterns of older households so that ownership and expenditure on goods such as PCs or CD players may be related to the presence of younger people in the household. One way of addressing this problem is to examine rates of ownership and expenditure on household goods in older households where children (of any age) are present and in those where no children are present. Our analysis of FES data shows that the rates of TV ownership are virtually identical for both types of households for all the years studied, reaching around 100% by 1983. Similarly, an examination of expenditure on household goods as a percentage of total expenditure reveals very little difference in the trends over time. It would appear therefore that the increase in ownership of consumer goods among older households is not being driven by the co-residence of younger members of those households.

Trends in consumption by the proportion of total household income accounted for by the state pension

It was noted at the beginning of this book that the last quarter of the 20th century witnessed considerable changes in the incomes of older people, reflecting a marked growth in real net pensioner income and a fall in the proportion of pensioners below the poverty line (Hills and Stewart, 2005). Between 1979 and 1996/97, pensioners' net income rose by 70% after housing costs in real terms compared with a growth of only 36% in real terms in average earnings in the whole economy (DWP, 2007). The emergence of a high-income group of older people on occupational pensions has been linked to a rise in income inequality among older groups (Hills, 2004). The evidence from our analysis of FES data is equivocal. If we look at patterns of ownership of goods such as fridge-freezers, we find that inequalities in ownership by pension income tend to disappear by the mid-1980s as ownership levels for certain goods reach 100% for all groups. However, if we consider the proportion of household expenditure spent on services (Figure 6.8) there is a clear, positive relationship in the early part of the period, so that the greater the proportion of income that is attributable to the state pension, the higher the proportion spent on services. Thus, in 1968, those who got between three quarters and all of their income from the state pension spent around 35% of their total expenditure on services compared with about 26% of those who derived less than a quarter of their income from the state pension. Although the proportions fell for all households, inequalities were evident across the period. By 2000/01, these figures were 26% and 17%, respectively.

Figure 6.8: Expenditure on services, by proportion of household income accounted for by pension income, 1968-2001

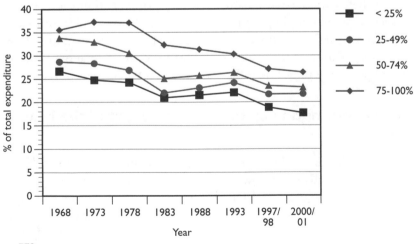

Source: FES

Trends in consumption by the type of housing tenure

Housing tenure (that is, whether someone is home owner or rents their property) has been shown to be associated with inequalities in health among older people (Breeze et al, 1999) and quality of life in old age (Blane et al, 2004; Wiggins et al, 2007). The UK has been referred to as a 'home-owning' democracy and has the highest rates of home ownership in Europe. Indeed, one only has to consider the number of televised home 'make-over' shows to grasp the cultural, and financial, importance of home ownership in this country. However, this has not always been the case. In the 1950s and 1960s, rates of home ownership were relatively low, at around 30%. By the end of the 20th century, this had increased to 67% (Holmans, 2000). Home-ownership levels have influenced patterns of wealth and assets among those cohorts of older people that have benefited from the long-term rise in house prices. In 1970, the ratio of house prices to earnings was 2.68. By 2006, this had risen to 4.76 (www.communities.gov.uk, Tables 517 and 801). However, at the time of writing, the consequences of this housing effect appear more uncertain as the effects of sub-prime mortgages begin to filter through from the US and younger cohorts face an increasingly uncertain future in terms of house prices and housing tenure. Thus, it is important to examine the impact of the shifts in housing tenure since the 1970s on consumption and expenditure among older households. Our analysis found that rates of car ownership are very different for those who own their home compared with those who rent. In 1968, only around 10% of those in rented accommodation owned a car, while 40% of owner-occupiers did so. Over time, although rates rise for both types of household, the gap remained fairly stable until 1993 when the rate of car ownership among rented households fell dramatically back down to 20% from a high of 40% in 1988. Thence recovery was slow and, by 2000/01, just under 30% of those in rented accommodation owned a car compared with around 70% of those who also owned their own accommodation. Turning to expenditure on fuel, again there are clear differences between the two types of household. Although the proportion spent on fuel declined over the period, at all points in time those in rented accommodation spent a higher proportion of their total expenditure on heating and powering their home than those who owned their property.

Trends in consumption by the pseudo cohort of the head of household

Our focus in this book has been on generational change and it is possible using the FES to examine changes in ownership and expenditure among age cohorts. Evidence from a study of age-related consumption patterns in France supports the assumption that differences in consumption between groups of older people are principally attributable to the different generational experiences of different cohorts (Ekert-Jaffé, 1989). It is important to recognise that the FES was a cross-sectional survey.Thus the cohorts examined in this analysis are made up of different households in each year and the analysis is referred to as a pseudo-cohort or quasi-cohort analysis (Evandrou and Falkingham, 2002). However, the data indicate that older households comprising younger cohorts do have different expenditure patterns to older households comprising older cohorts. Looking at Figure 6.9, two things are apparent. First, there are clear inter-cohort differences. At each point in time for which we have data, those in the younger cohorts have higher rates of car ownership than those in the older cohorts. For example, in 1973, only 20% of those households where the head of household was born between 1896 and 1900 owned a car compared with over 40% of those households where the head of household was born between 1911 and 1915. Second, there are some interesting intra-cohort patterns. For almost every cohort, there is an increase in the rates of car ownership as time goes by.Thus among those born between 1926 and 1920, the rates of ownership rise from around 35% in 1978 to close to 70% in 1983. However, this rise is followed by a fall for all cohorts.This could be possible evidence of an age effect within these cohorts, so that as members of the cohort age they give up car ownership due to possible health or financial limitations. Another explanation is that we could be seeing another expression of the gender differences witnessed in Figure 6.5. Given greater female life expectancy, as cohorts age, mortality is not randomly distributed by sex and it is the men who die off.

Figure 6.9: Ownership of a car, by pseudo-cohort of HoH, 1973-2001

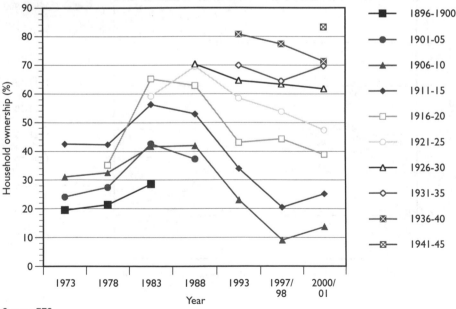

Source: FES

A significant number of women who do not own a car may be found within older cohorts. Turning to the proportion of expenditure spent on clothing (Figure 6.10) for these cohorts, no discernible pattern of inter-cohort differences can be identified. There is some evidence that for earlier cohorts there was a relatively stable trend in expenditure, while for later cohorts there is a general downward trend. At each time point, however, especially from the early 1980s onwards, there are no real differences between each of the cohorts.

The data we have presented here indicate convergence, stasis and increasing inequalities in the consumption patterns of older households. This is consistent with our earlier finding that over time the ownership of key consumer items by different sections of the retired population converges and becomes similar to that of working-age households. However, patterns of inequality persist between older households so that as patterns of expenditure change we may be witnessing a deepening of exclusion for some pensioner groups particularly women in older cohorts.

During the 1950s, social researchers such as Abrams (1951) regarded the economic circumstances of older people as to be so low as to necessitate their exclusion from any analysis of consumption. However, the circumstances of the different cohorts of people entering retirement during the second half of 20th century changed the experiences of retirement as newer retirees had benefited from the rise in standards of living more than those who had retired before them,

Figure 6.10: Expenditure on clothing as a proportion of total expenditure, by pseudo-cohort of HoH, 1968-2001

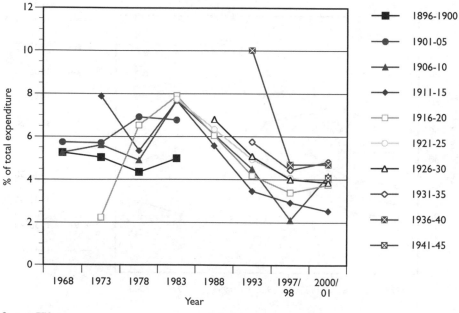

Source: FES

due to increased returns on occupational pensions, greater home ownership and more dual-earner families. These changes had such a significant impact that by 2001 the income distribution of the retired population as a whole became more closely matched to that of the working-age population than it did to other groups such as the unemployed or lone parents with children. Paradoxically, this also meant that there are wider disparities of income between the better-off and the worse-off retired as later life begins to reflect more closely the greater inequalities of society at large (Jackson, 2006). The UK may therefore be experiencing a transformation of the field of ageing as cohorts who grew up in relative prosperity become used to that relative affluence and bring into later life a generational habitus of consumption. These trends are certainly being encouraged by the British government as it seeks to reduce its commitments to funding later life. Mann (2006) argues that the UK government is increasingly using the language of consumption in articulating its pensions and retirement policies. Rather than retirement being a government responsibility, it is now seen as belonging to the arena of the active citizen consumer and lifestyle manager. Those who wish to remain as 'passive welfare recipients' lose out all of the way whether this is in terms of income or in terms of being seen as 'passive'. People in retirement find that they are incorporated into the processes of consumption and the imperatives of consumer society. By unpicking the rise of older people's engagement with consumer society, it is possible to show that older households are heterogeneous and their capacity to participate in this new consumer-oriented social order is uneven.

Conclusion

It will be obvious to many readers that the various socio-demographic factors that have been looked at in this chapter, although logically independent, are highly interconnected. For example, most of those who are unmarried in later life are widows, as women outlive men on average, and widows often have the poorest economic circumstances, due to the gendered division of labour and lower labour market participation rates for women in these 'older' cohorts. Sex, cohort, health, household tenure, marital status and income all come together in complex and historically unique ways to produce disadvantage. The intention in this chapter was to show that even at a simple descriptive level – the relative proportions of their expenditures spent on different categories of consumption – the retired population not only participate in consumer society, but, in doing so, come to reflect many of the patterns and divisions present in wider society. Further work is needed to investigate the inter-relationship between cohorts, gender and retirement as well as the structure of households on the patterns of expenditures we have described. By doing so, will we be able to deepen our understanding of how later life is being transformed by the generational habitus of consumer society.

SEVEN

Consuming health in later life

Introduction

In this book, we have so far looked at a number of different aspects of the role of consumption in shaping the identity and experience of later life in contemporary Britain. Here we focus on health and health-related consumption. This is a rather different entity from those considered in earlier chapters where we looked at the growth of access to material goods by older people. Clearly, goods such as washing machines, videos and computers need little explanation or justification as 'consumption items'. They are material objects that have both a physical form and convey a variety (or myriad) of meanings about identity, aesthetics and the consumer's sense of self. However, consumption is not only limited to the arena of tangible goods, but is also concerned with services (both tangible and intangible), leisure pursuits and 'lifestyles'. Gould and Gould (2001) argue that intangibles such as health, not just healthcare, as well as tangibles can be conceptualised as consumption goods. Hence the study of health consumption involves a broad spectrum of activity, including the provision (and consumption of) goods and services, the development of health-related lifestyles and the experience and distribution of 'health' within and between populations. We therefore can examine health (care) practices via the perspective of consumption as a means of understanding health inequalities within and between specific social groups.

This proposition of health as a consumption good is not without its problems, particularly when we consider the extent to which health is produced and maintained by individuals, groups and communities. However, in the context of the growth of consumerism and choice as dominant motifs in the development of health and welfare policy, it is important to consider the extent to which the construction of older people as citizen consumers is linked to an increasingly individualised pattern of consumption of health and healthcare (Gilleard and Higgs, 1998). As we will see in the next chapter, the National Health Service (NHS) has become increasingly dominated by notions of (quasi-) markets, competition between providers, the development of commissioning (purchasing of services) and the development of the voice of the consumer (previously users or patients). Calnan and Gabe (2001) suggest that the focus on consumerism and user choice may have emerged as a response to consumer movements. In the UK, these pressures developed through the activities of the Consumers' Association and specific patient groups, based as they were on the emulation and adaptation of consumerist ideas from North America. In parallel with an increasing emphasis on choice and consumerism, successive governments have promoted a user-involvement/citizen-participation agenda in the healthcare arena. This has taken a variety of forms over the years; the latest manifestation is the development of Patient Advice and Liaison Services (PALS) and community and patient forums. Evidence regarding the success of these initiatives is, at best, mixed. They certainly appear to be a highly limited and prescribed form of citizen participation, but there is some evidence that they have had an influence on organisational changes, for example in geriatric services (Milewa et al, 1999). Overall, however, it is clear that the emphasis in healthcare has shifted from citizens with a collective voice to citizens as individual consumers. The rhetoric is around choice and the empowerment of users, even if the reality falls some way short of this aspiration on the part of policy makers.

In this chapter, we examine the development of health-based consumption and the emergence of a healthcare and lifestyle market. While the focus is on older people, the data used relate to the general adult population and as such many of the points made have a wider resonance. To provide a background to the analysis, we begin with a brief overview of the health of older people and their use of health services. Then, using available data, we examine the development of the post-war healthcare market, the development of health-related consumption and expenditure on health and health-related services by older people, examining trends for the period 1973-2000/01. We then contrast household expenditure on health and health-related services in the UK with expenditure in the United States.

Health and healthcare and older people

Before examining the development of explicit health-based consumption patterns among older people, it is important to contextualise these substantive topics by considering the health of older people and their utilisation of health services. As argued above, we see both the distribution of health within the older population and their utilisation of formal healthcare services as elements of a broader analysis of the consumption of health. There is an extensive body of work enumerating the trends in morbidity and health status of older people, the incidence and prevalence of specific diseases and the 'consumption' of publicly funded 'health goods' within the context of a universal healthcare system. Additionally, these trends are often linked to the concern with overall health-related expenditure and implications of population ageing. While we do not wish to enter these debates in detail, some examination of these issues provides the context for our focus on consumption and the development of health-related lifestyles among the older population. Our physical and mental health inevitably influences our ability to 'consume' regardless of age. Conceptually, we might propose that poor health might increase our consumption because of the need to purchase health-related goods and services to compensate/ameliorate for health deficits. Alternatively, poor health can reduce consumption because of the constraints imposed on our ability to spend both in terms of levels of income and the ability to access markets.

Rather than consider the epidemiology of specific conditions, we focus here on the types of conditions experienced by older people and how that contextualises their use of health services and, potentially, their ability to participate in healthcare consumption. Two key features differentiate the health experiences of young and old: the prevalence of chronic illness and the extent of multiple pathology. Table 7.1 shows that between 1981 and 2002 there were marked increases in life expectancy for males and females. Healthy life expectancy and disability-free life expectancy also increased, but not to the same degree (Self and Zealey, 2007). These data are based on self-reported levels of general health and limiting long-standing illness and exclude the most frail not living in the community; hence, these estimates should be treated with some degree of caution. However, they suggest that the improvements in terms of longevity may contain a sting in the tail in that this longevity is accompanied by poor levels of health and higher levels of disability.

As noted, however, care must be taken when interpreting these data. For example, previous analysis showed that life expectancy for men aged 85 and over increased from 4.3 years to 5.3 years between 1980 and 1998, while over the same period disability-free life expectancy increased from 2.7 years to 4.2 years (Evandrou, 2005). These data suggest a very different scenario where the proportion of remaining life lived disability-free rose significantly, some 50%, over the last 20 years of the 20th century.

Regardless of the precise nature of the measure used – long-term limiting illness, disability or long-term conditions – the pattern is the same: rates of chronic health problems increase with age. Furthermore, the number of 'long-term' conditions experienced by individuals also increases with age. If we examine key dimensions of the health status of older people, we find that there is some variation with age and gender, with both men and women showing decreasing rates of diagnosed mental illness with age while rates of dementia increase rapidly with age (ADI,

Table 7.1: Life expectancy, healthy life expectancy and disability-free life expectancy at birth, by sex (Great Britain)

	Males		Females	
	1981	2002	1981	2002
Life expectancy	70.9	76.0	76.8	80.5
Healthy life expectancy	64.4	67.2	66.7	69.9
Years spent in poor health	6.4	8.8	10.1	10.6
Disability-free life expectancy	58.1	60.9	60.8	63
Years spent with disability	12.8	15.0	16.0	17.5

Source: www.statistics.gov.uk

1999). Rates of self-reported limiting long-term illness increase with age and are higher among men than women at older ages. In contrast, rates of diagnosed arthritis also increase with age, but, in this instance, rates are higher among women (Marmot et al, 2003). Such data serve to illustrate that, with the exception of some illnesses (for example, mental illness), the greatest healthcare 'needs' are located within this segment of the population. It is also important to note that, for older people, the pattern of healthcare needs is very different from that presented by younger age groups, which, typically, present with a single healthcare problem. We may speculate that this has implications for how the older person experiences the healthcare system. Clearly, the model of choice and involved decision making is more problematic when being applied to a 'consumer group' experiencing a number of different health conditions simultaneously. Furthermore, healthcare systems are usually predicated on the treatment of single conditions. Hence when older users (or patients) arrive in acute hospital settings, they are often labelled as 'inappropriate' because they do not fit neatly into the service template designed for the diagnosis and treatment of 'single-condition' diseases. It is with these basic trends in mind that we should consider the commodification of health and healthcare and the development of the healthcare markets.

The development of healthcare markets

Although the creation of the NHS in 1948 effectively nationalised the vast majority of existing healthcare infrastructure and the majority of the staff became employees of the state, a large section of the NHS (general practice) retained its status as an independent contractor. In addition, there remained a vestigial private healthcare sector predominantly focusing on maternity, convalescence and some routine elective surgical procedures. There were also 'private' pay beds within NHS hospitals. However, most hospital care, general practitioner consultations and referrals, and hospital inpatient and outpatient episodes were encompassed by the new NHS and were essentially free at the point of delivery. Hence, access to, and utilisation of, healthcare was decoupled from the ability to pay, an important development for low-income groups such as older people predominantly living on not overly generous pensions. It is not within the remit of this book to review the development of private healthcare provision. However, in looking at the development of health-based consumption identity among older people (and indeed younger ones), we need to take into account two related trends. First, especially in the post-1990 period, there has been the growth of 'markets' within the NHS, as illustrated by a string of initiatives including fund-holding GP practices, followed by a move towards commissioning within primary care trusts, the development of 'private' facilities (such as diagnostic and treatment facilities) to treat NHS patients, and the emphasis on 'choice' (in terms of place and date) in hospital care (see chapter eight for further discussion of these developments). Second, allied to the 'marketisation' of the NHS, there is the continued presence of private healthcare services at primary care level (for example, optical and dental services) as well as secondary care level. This is combined with the development of 'lifestyle' healthcare interventions, including a variety of health-promoting alternative therapies and, increasingly, cosmetic surgery.

Conditions that were once considered incurable or seen as an inevitable part of old age, such as arthritis of the hip, have, in the course of two generations, been recalibrated as 'curable' diseases, many of which are ameliorated by a routine procedure. Hip replacement is now part of 'normal' orthopaedic practice and has demonstrable benefit in terms of maintaining the independence of older people and promoting their quality of life. The National Audit Office (NAO, 2000) reported that the NHS in England undertook some 30,000 hip operations a year, in 207 acute hospital trusts, at a total cost of £140 million and an average cost of £3,700 per procedure (range of £384 to £7,784 depending on complexity of the operation, length of hospital stay and choice of prosthesis). The expectation of a hip replacement at some time in later life has become a normalising experience. While we might not view this as 'anti-ageing' medicine, joint replacements and increased surgical and medical therapies for the treatment and management of debilitating conditions such as arthritis, stroke and heart disease offer opportunities for enhanced quality of life and have made significant contributions to the increases in life expectancy experienced in the past quarter century.

The example of hip replacements serves to illustrate the development of different aspects of the expanding healthcare market in the treatment of diseases of later life. The NAO report notes the development of a thriving market in hip prostheses (citing 63 different types being used in the NHS in England), but also there are growth markets in the development of medical devices (blood pressure and glucose monitors), 'anti-brain-ageing' drugs (for example, Aricept, Donezepil and Rivastigmine) and assistive technologies such as global positioning satellite location systems that are marketed to both promote the safety and security of older people and of their carers. Some of these technologies may have clear and measurable benefits for older people, while others reflect fervent aspirations more than achieved outcomes, and still others are part of a general trend towards the medicalisation and surveillance of 'old age'. Whether they are purchased through the NHS or privately, they represent a large and growing part of corporate interest (pharmaceutical companies, medical technology companies and private healthcare providers) in ageing and later life.

We must also note the growth of complimentary medicine and alternative therapies, the emergence of 'health foods' and the marketing of food supplements and vitamins aimed at the 'older' consumer. Therapies such as acupuncture, aromatherapy and reflexology all fall within the healthcare consumption orbit. Generally, these are 'private' services for which users pay either in cash or via insurance policies. Prescribed medicines in the UK are available free of charge to those over the age of 60. Non-prescription medicines use by older people is therefore low relative to some other countries. As a consequence, few studies have investigated the use of non-prescription medicines, over-the-counter medicines and complementary and alternative medicines (CAMs) by older people. Where such medicines have been included in studies, they have not been separated from prescription medicines in the analysis (Chen et al, 2001; Andrews, 2002). However, there is some evidence to suggest that older people choose to self-treat with a wide range of non-prescription medicines, even though these come at a price (McElnay and Dickson, 1994; Poole et al, 1999). Various studies from Denmark, Canada and Sweden indicate that older people do self-treat with a range of such medicines (Al-Windi et al, 2000; Barat et al, 2000; Ballantyne et al, 2005). Furthermore, while it would appear reasonable to assume that the expense of health products would tend to deter older people from their consumption, there is some evidence of equivalent levels of use of CAMs by older people compared with younger groups (Ernest and White, 2000). There is a strand in the literature that hints that ageing baby boomers will contribute to trends towards increasing use of non-prescription medicines (Thomas et al, 2001; Andrews, 2002). It may be that older consumers turn to these different forms of non-prescription medicines and health products in response to perceived failings of the formal health sector. For example, older users of homeopathy have reported dissatisfaction with mainstream geriatric medicine (Conway and Hockey, 1998) and older patients seeking CAMs have reported this is in response to the lack of success of conventional care in addressing chronic health conditions (Wellman et al, 2001). The greater attention and longer 'consultations' offered by alternative practitioners may be a factor in the decision to use such services. Kelner and Wellman (1997) suggest that the increasing use of CAMs by older people reflects a greater number of 'smart customers' with more individualised consumer-oriented approaches to their healthcare. Furthermore, it is not an 'either or' choice. Older people appear to adopt a pluralistic approach to non-prescription medicines, combining them with their use of orthodox treatments (Andrews, 2003).

In addition to trends in complementary and alternative medicine, we must also note services such as physiotherapy that can be purchased within the private sector, used via health insurance or provided within the NHS. In combination, these trends provide a context whereby health is increasingly seen as a good that can be purchased and healthcare use is not simply limited to the services provided by the NHS. A wider variety of different goods and services are available and the barrier between private and public provision has become much more porous. We can identify similar trends in the provision of social care, where services once provided by the state, via local authorities, are now offered by the private sector (see the next chapter for further discussion on this point). It is important to note, however, that charges have always been an integral component of the provision of social care.

Healthcare consumption

We can examine the use of health services made by older people in several different ways. We can consider what component of healthcare is accounted for by older people and we can consider the percentage of older people using different types of healthcare services. We consider both approaches here. Data from the Wanless report (Wanless, 2006) indicate that those aged 65 and over account for 35% of elective admissions (50% of elective bed days) and 40% of emergency admissions (63% of emergency bed days). There is an important distinction between elective and emergency admissions that is not simply confined to statistical niceties. Elective admissions relate to those where the procedure is planned and anticipated; typical of this type of admission are joint replacement procedures. Here we can see that those aged 65 and over are not the main consumer group for this type of procedure in terms of admissions, but older people tend to experience longer lengths of stay.

In terms of utilisation, older people are a major group using the services provided by the health and social care system within the UK. In 2002/03, among people aged 50 and over, 20% had consulted a GP in the previous two weeks. Over the previous 12 months, 20% had attended an outpatient or casualty department, 10% had had a hospital inpatient stay and 8% had attended as a day patient (Evandrou, 2005). As expected, use of healthcare services varied by age, with individuals in older age groups being more likely to seek medical attention than those in the younger age groups. From this perspective, older people are the largest single 'consumer' group for the services provided by the NHS. However, it is something of a conceptual leap to move from the rhetoric of utilisation, which is redolent of the ideology of the 'state-provided' healthcare system, to that of consumer, with all the implied notions of choice and markets and, perhaps, of 'discretionary' expenditure. When thinking about products and services that we can choose to purchase, items such as consumer durables, holidays or gym membership are easily encompassed within this category. Similarly, purchases such as 'health foods' or cosmetic surgery such as facelifts, to remove signs of ageing, can be so classified. However, this analogy does not fit so well with acute healthcare episodes such as strokes or heart attacks where decisions about hospital admission are less easily categorised as discretionary, although there may be choices, which the government is now actively promoting, as to which hospital to attend. How much of this consumption is accounted for by the private sector? Propper (2000), using British Household Panel data, estimates that approximately 20% of the population use private healthcare. However, this is largely accounted for by the use of dental (11%) and optical (13%) services, with 5% reporting the use of private physiotherapy and 1% private inpatient care. Hence, the bulk of the private healthcare market is focused on the primary care-type services of dentistry and optical services where NHS provision is sparse and consumption of private sector services is, perhaps, more out of necessity than 'true choice'.

Healthcare expenditure

In previous chapters, we have seen how the Family Expenditure Survey (FES) provides a barometer that reflects the development of the post-war consumer society as it charts the fall and rise of expenditure on specific types of consumer goods and services. For example, items such as black-and-white televisions are no longer included in the survey, but mobile phones and MP3 players are recent additions. Similar changes are evident in fashion, foods and entertainment/leisure and the emergence of whole new areas of expenditure such as motoring-related speeding fines. Naturally, when charting these changes, we must note that these apply to the general population as a whole, not just older people. FES data have, since the initial survey in 1953, included a variety of different health-related measures. These have varied in their precise location in the interview schedules and datasets, making analysis of expenditure specific to health technically complex, a complexity that is compounded by subtle changes in the definitions of apparently identical variables. Location within the FES dataset offers some insight into how health-related goods and services are conceptualised by the survey commissioners. Up until 2001/02, health services were classified as 'personal services'. This category includes medicines, prescriptions and spectacles; medical, dental, optical and nursing fees; toiletries and soap; cosmetics; beauty treatments; and leather and jewellery goods. Since 2001/02, however, expenditures have been regrouped, with the formation of a discrete (but not exhaustive) category of 'health' to facilitate comparison with expenditure budget studies across Europe. Given these caveats, what does the FES tell us about health-related consumption by the population of Britain in the post war period? As Box 7.1 shows, the FES has consistently recorded expenditure on two main areas of health-related activity: medical goods and appliances; and medical, dental and nursing fees. Hence, it is an 'ever-present' item of expenditure.

Box 7.1: The major areas of health-related expenditure included in the Family Expenditure Survey

From 1953 until 2001, healthcare expenditure was categorised thus:

- Medicines, drugs, lotions and surgical goods; non-NHS and NHS prescriptions; opticians', dentists' and hospital charges (including NHS pay beds)
- Medical, dental and nursing fees (spectacles added in 1987); distinguishing private and NHS payments
- Subscriptions to 'sick clubs' included until 1972; medical insurance included from 1978 as a distinct category

---

Since 2001, healthcare expenditure has been recorded thus:

- Medical products, appliances and equipment:
  - medicines, prescriptions and healthcare products
  - NHS prescription charges and payments
  - medicines and medical goods (not NHS)
  - other medical products
  - spectacles, lenses, accessories and repairs
  - purchase of spectacles, lenses, prescription sunglasses
  - accessories/repairs to spectacles/lenses
  - non-optical appliances and equipment
  - outpatient services
  - NHS medical, optical, dental and medical auxiliary services
  - private medical, optical, dental and medical auxiliary services
  - other services
  - inpatient hospital services
- Social protection
- Residential homes and home help
- Medical insurance premiums

In addition, the initial survey recorded contributions made towards 'Friendly Society' and accident injury medical expenses insurance. However, non-NHS expenditure on spectacles was recorded under the optical and photographic expenditure category. Integral to these two major forms of health-related expenditure is the distinction between contributions towards NHS services and expenditure on 'privately provided' goods and services. This essential architecture of data collection has remained, although there have been additions of items of expenditure such as contact lenses in 1994 and prescription sunglasses in 1992 and a discrete medical insurance category in 1979. In addition, there have been subtle alterations in what is included within categories, such as the movement of expenditure on private spectacles from optical and photographic to the medical and surgical goods category in 1987. We can also see this in the emergence of 'social protection' items in the types of expenditure recorded by the FES. Since 2001, information has been collected on care home expenditure and home help services (as well as childcare, which is also included within this category). This reflects the emergence of new forms of health-related expenditure, either individuals taking on expenditure for goods or services previously provided by the NHS/social care agencies or the development of new products. So, since 2001, we can chart the growth of expenditure on nursing home care and on home helps. While both of these services have always existed in the private sector, until the mid-1990s the primary provider of domiciliary home care and residential homes was the state. We can see the retrenchment of the state as a provider of services in other routine data sets. The General Household Survey (GHS), a general survey of the population, has conducted five specific surveys of the population aged 65 and over living in the community. In 1985, respondents were asked if they received a home help. No distinction was made between help provided by the local authority or privately arranged help. By 1991, the two types of provider were differentiated; by 1998, the private sector was the largest provider and by 2001, 10% of those aged 65+ received a private home help and 4% a local authority one. This reliance on private sector provision is greatest among the very old (those aged 85 and over) and women, with 35% of women aged 85 and over receiving private home help services. As with the primary care-based optical and dental services, it is unclear how much of this use of private services is a positive choice and how much a reaction to decreased availability of public provision.

When examining healthcare expenditure, we can undertake this analysis at two levels. First, we can consider macro-level national aggregate analyses looking at overall patterns of expenditure. We can also look at expenditure at the household (or individual) level. In this section, we present both levels of analyses, as these approaches are complementary. This is a topic where the application of a temporal perspective is very enlightening. However, examining temporal trends is problematic because of changes in definitions, the inclusion/exclusion of variables in the analysis and changes in sampling and methodology. At the most macro level, we can examine health spending in terms of the gross domestic product of a specific country. This, of course, does not relate directly to health outcomes but is an indicator of the amount of wealth within a country directed towards health-related activities. As we noted earlier in the chapter, older people in Britain are the main users of 'traditional' healthcare services and this inevitably raises concerns about the economic aspects of population ageing. This has prompted researchers to examine patterns of expenditure on healthcare per head of population. In a variety of different countries, healthcare expenditure shows a *j*-shaped distribution. It is expensive being born and then expenditure per head increases significantly in old age. This mirrors the well-established age-related trends in mortality and morbidity. However, a number of scholars (Seshamani and Gray, 2004; Johnson and Young, 2006) have shown that it is not age that is the important driver in increasing expenditure. They report that the 1% of the population that died in 2002 in England accounted for almost 29% of healthcare (hospital) costs. For the population aged 65+, the 5% of deaths generated almost a half of all the hospital costs for that age group. For our UK population group, none of these expenses is incurred personally and users do not have to seek reimbursement for 'up-front' expenses. This is very different from many other countries and is a key feature of the welfare state.

Overall, however, how much of their income do the population and in particular older groups within the UK population spend on healthcare? This is a somewhat complex question to answer, as those of working age and in employment are paying for healthcare via their taxes and national insurance contributions. However,

FES data do allow some global estimates of overall 'out-of-pocket' expenditure on healthcare. Self and Zealey (2007) estimate that in 2005 households in the UK spent £125 billion on positive, direct, health-related expenditures. This does not include health-promoting activities or food and drink. They also report that £28 billion was spent on items with a proven 'negative' health outcome, notably tobacco and alcoholic drinks. In percentage terms, the amount on expenditure on health has increased from 1% in 1971 to 2% in 2005 (Self and Zealey, 2007) and on tobacco and alcoholic drinks there has been a decrease from 7% of household expenditure to 4%.

Figure 7.1 shows that between the mid-1970s and the turn of the century, there were significant changes in the proportion of household expenditure spent on certain goods and services, with a major decline in the proportion spent on food and non-alcoholic drink mirrored by a large increase in the proportion spent on leisure goods and services. The proportion spent on personal goods and services was consistently around 4% throughout the period. This category includes medicines, prescriptions and spectacles; medical, dental, optical and nursing fees; toiletries and soap; cosmetics; beauty treatment; and leather and jewellery goods.

Looking at spending on personal goods and services, therefore, it would appear that, despite evidence of a shift towards consumption-based culture in the NHS and the conscious policy of developing and involving the private sector, trends in household expenditure on personal goods and services have remained low.

Figure 7.1: Trends in household expenditure on commodities and services as a percentage of all expenditure groups, 1974-2001

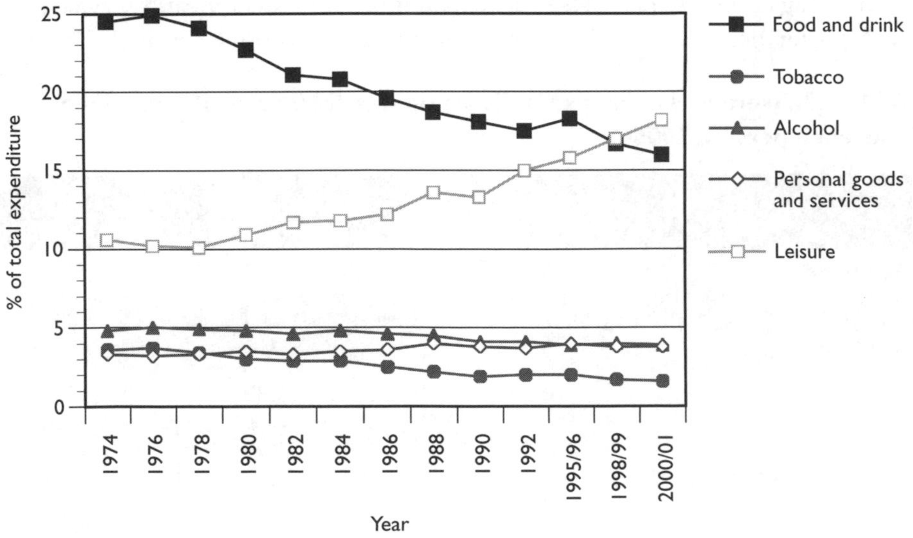

Source: ONS (2002a)

In 1953/54, 'pensioner households' (defined as those receiving state retirement benefits) spent 0.13% of their income on direct health-related expenditure and Friendly Society subscriptions. We can compare this with the situation in 2005, where households where older people were dominant were spending about 2% of income on direct health items (including insurance). Again, comparisons are difficult, but it seems clear that although in absolute terms expenditure has increased, health-related expenditure remains a minor item in the budgets of older people overall. However, there is clearly scope to examine differential patterns of expenditure within different sub-groups of the older population.

In 2005/06, the average household spent £5.50 per week on directly health-related expenditure, as included in the direct 'health' expenditure category described above, and medical products accounted for £3 of this (see Table 7.2). To this can be added a further £1.60 per week on health insurance, representing only 3% of the average weekly total household expenditure. These figures are almost certainly an underestimate, as it seems likely that some of the expenditure categorised as domestic cleaning and gardening services may well have a strong social protection/health element. In addition, there are expenditures on 'lifestyle' and health-maintenance activities and 'health lifestyle' products, such as health foods and organic produce, that are not separately recorded.

When considering household expenditure patterns of older people, there are a number of different ways that we can present the data. We can consider the analysis in terms of the age of the index household member or households where the reference interviewee self-reports as retired. Clearly, these categories overlap but are not coterminous. Here, we have looked at the data from both perspectives and, while there are differences of nuance, the broad pattern is very similar. Data from the 2005/06 FES show that the average household headed by a person aged 65-74 spent 4% of its expenditure on 'direct' health services and health insurance (see Table 7.2). This percentage demonstrates remarkably little

Table 7.2: Average weekly expenditure on health, by age of household reference person, 2005-06

	Less than 30	30-49	50-64	65-74	75+	All households
Health	2.10	6.00	6.90	5.30	3.70	5.50
Medical products, appliances and equipment	1.40	2.90	3.70	3.60	2.40	3.00
Hospital services	0.60	3.10	3.20	1.80	1.40	2.50
Health insurance	0.30	1.20	2.50	2.10	1.70	1.60
Total weekly expenditure (%)	1.4	3.9	4.4	4.1	3.7	3.8

Source: ONS (2006)

variability with age but, again, is inevitably an underestimate of the domains we wish to measure for the reasons noted above.

If we look in more detail at household expenditure by age of the household reference person (Table 7.3), we can see that recreation and culture remain a significant proportion of household expenditure even in households aged 75 and over (12.6% compared with 13% for all households). The main declines in the proportionate spend in older households appear to be in the areas of restaurants and hotels, transport and other items, while the proportionate increase appears to be located in food and housing. While the actual amounts are small, there is some evidence from these data that even those well into 'retirement' are using their income to participate in leisure-based activities. This suggests that older people today are spending their income in very different ways from their counterparts in 1953/54, when there was virtually no expenditure on 'non-essential' goods or services.

If we compare retired households with non-retired households, we can see considerable differences in expenditure on health, with retired households on state pensions spending on average £2.50 a week on health, while 'other' retired spend an average £4.75 a week. Non-retired households spend an average £6.15 a week (ONS, 2007a, Table A25). These figures suggest that there are variations both between retired and non-retired households and within retired households. This

Table 7.3: Household expenditure as a percentage of total expenditure, by age of household reference person, 2005-06, UK

	50-64	65-74	75 and over	All housesholds
Food and non-alcoholic drinks	10.5	13.0	15.0	10.2
Alcoholic drinks, tobacco and narcotics	2.7	2.8	2.2	2.4
Clothing and footwear	4.8	4.6	3.5	5.1
Housing, fuel and power	8.5	10.1	14.5	10.0
Household goods and services	6.8	8.7	9.1	6.8
Health	1.4	1.7	1.8	1.2
Transport	15.0	14.1	8.7	13.9
Communication	2.6	2.3	2.6	2.7
Recreation and culture	13.7	16.0	12.6	13.0
Education	1.2	0.1	0.8	1.5
Restaurants and hotels	8.2	7.4	6.2	8.3
Miscellaneous goods and services	7.6	7.8	10.7	7.8
Other expenditure items	16.9	11.5	12.2	17.1

Source: ONS (2006, Table A11)

remains an area where there is considerable scope for further research. There is also considerable scope to undertake detailed analyses of the expenditure patterns of older people both in terms of comparisons with those from different age groups and, importantly, in terms of differentials within the older age groups of age, class, ethnicity and gender. If we look, for example, at household expenditure by gross income quintile group among people aged 65-74, we can see that there are inequalities in both total expenditure and in expenditure on health and recreation, both in absolute terms and as a proportion of total expenditure (Table 7.4). Expenditure on health averages £2.50 in the lowest quintile, rising sixfold to £17.80 in the highest quintile. Expenditure on recreation and culture averages £20.70 in the lowest quintile, rising fivefold to £112.70 in the highest quintile. As a proportion of total expenditure, it appears that health spending shows a steady gradient, while spending on recreation and culture follows a more varied trajectory. Despite the increasing availability of such data, there is still comparatively little work on this aspect of later life, perhaps partly because of the emphasis on where income is derived from rather than how people use their income.

How have health-related expenditure patterns changed over time? Analysis of data for the period 1973-2000/01 enables us to look at general trends within the population and, more specifically, older households. There has been little increase in the percentage of income that the population as a whole spends on health-related goods. However, within this overall situation of stability, it would appear that the proportion spent on NHS-related services almost tripled between 1973 and 2000, while spending on private healthcare fell by a similar proportion. If we look at households by the age of the head of household for 1973 and 2000/01, we can see that in the early 1970s spending was broadly similar between younger and older households, with some higher spending among older households showing through in private healthcare expenditure. However, by 2000/01, the proportionate spend on total health expenditure had increased

Table 7.4: Household expenditure by gross income quintile group where the household reference person is aged 65-74, 2003/04-2005/06

	Quintiles					
	Lowest	Second	Third	Fourth	Highest	All
Health	2.50	4.30	6.50	9.20	17.80	5.40
Recreation and culture	20.70	43.30	65.50	77.60	112.70	47.80
Total expenditure	153.60	259.30	380.00	483.00	734.00	297.70
Health as % of total	1.6	1.7	1.7	1.9	2.4	1.8
Recreation and culture as % of total	13.5	16.7	17.2	16.1	15.4	16.1

Source: ONS (2006, Table A17)

for older households and this is linked to an increase in the proportion of NHS spending by this older group (see Figure 7.2).

Figure 7.2: Mean total health expenditure and NHS and private health expenditure as a proportion of total expenditure for households where HoH is aged 60 and over or aged under 60, 1973 and 2000-01

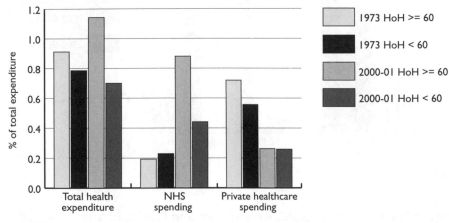

Source: FES

As we have argued, it is important to examine consumption patterns in terms of how older people compare with the rest of the population and in terms of how expenditure varies within this population. Within the broad trends of a very modest increase in expenditure in health-related expenditure for older households and an expenditure shift from private healthcare to NHS healthcare, Figure 7.3 suggests that, by 2000/01, households headed by older women spent more of their income on health compared with those headed by older men. This is a reversal of the picture in 1973. Although the percentages remain small, the turnaround is sufficient to warrant further research in this area.

Similarly, when we examine expenditure trends by income quartile over time, we find that the modest increase in health-related expenditure is most evident among those in the top two income quartiles (Figures 7.4 and 7.5). The expenditure patterns for 200/01 show a more obvious income-related gradient than in 1973. Furthermore, there is some suggestion that this gradient has become more visible in terms of the proportionate NHS spend.

We anticipate that this area of research will grow as social gerontologists (and sociologists of later life) focus on how older people spend their money, not as an alternative to, but in conjunction with, studies of income and wealth in later life. We also anticipate the research potential for examining consumption patterns over the lifecycle. How do patterns change over time? Which elements of consumption are

Figure 7.3: Mean total health expenditure and NHS and private health expenditure as a proportion of total expenditure for households by sex of HoH for those aged 60, 1973 and 2000-01

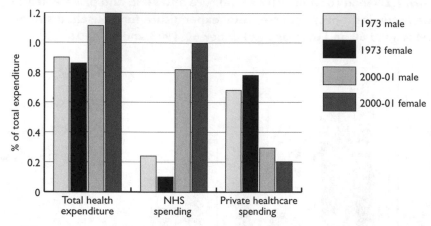

Source: FES

Figure 7.4: Mean total health expenditure and NHS and private health expenditure as a proportion of total expenditure for households, by equivalised income quintile (McClements Scale) of HoH for those aged 60, 1973

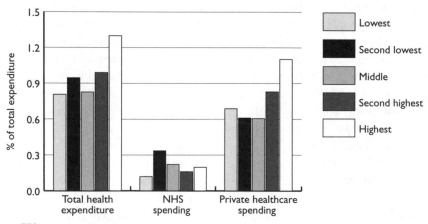

Source: FES

retained in later life, which new consumption patterns emerge and which aspects decline? For example, we would argue that gym membership and participation in health- and exercise-based activities represents a very different form of 'health consumption' from gardening; although the latter is clearly important as a form of exercise, it is not necessarily a consciously lifestyle or health-promoting

Figure 7.5: Mean total health expenditure and NHS and private health expenditure as a proportion of total expenditure for households, by equivalised income quintile (McClements Scale) of HoH for those aged 60, 2000-01

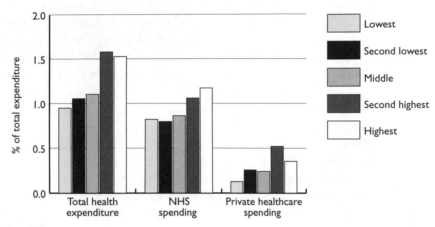

Source: FES

activity. Data on exercise participation rates are both problematic, being largely based on self-report, and limited in their coverage. The 2002 GHS (ONS 2004) reports that in the four weeks before interview between 5% and 6% of those aged 60 and over had been swimming and a similar percentage to a keep fit class (attending a gym was not included in the list of potential activities). So, while far from universal, a group of older people appears to be emerging who participate in exercise and uses their financial resources to support this activity. Data from the Sport England Active People Survey for 2005/06 (www.sportengland.org) show that here is a small sub-group of highly active older people who not only participate and volunteer in sports and fitness but also actively compete (or take part) in mass participation and competitive events. At the 2007 London marathon, there were 529 finishers aged 65 years and over and there are significant levels of participations in veterans'/masters' competitions across a range of sports within Britain and internationally. There is a rich research agenda here, looking at the extent of older people's participation in leisure and sporting-related activities and their motivations for this. Is this a manifestation of the continuation of an established lifestyle, a way of resisting or denying old age or the ultimate manifestation of the active ageing theory?

Comparisons with the US

In this brief overview, we have shown some trends in expenditure on health-related goods and services by older people. It is possible to discern the development of expenditure patterns and consumption that relate to health-related lifestyles and activities and there is some evidence of inequalities in expenditure in these areas among older groups. We suggest that there is considerable scope to develop this research agenda, especially in terms of examining the relationship between measures of social location, gender and age-based differentials in these types of expenditure. These trends need to be seen in the context of the NHS, which remains an almost unique system of organising the delivery of healthcare to a population, especially in terms of the virtually comprehensive nature of the services covered by acute hospital care and primary medical care (although less so for optical and dental care). How does health consumption figure as a component of the expenditure of older people in other countries? In the US, those aged 65 years and over are eligible to receive health services via the Medicare service (www.medicare.gov). The rules are complex, but the general principle is that people aged 65+ with an appropriate employment record are eligible for 'part A' coverage, which includes hospital inpatient episodes (minus a contribution). Part B coverage requires a monthly premium and relates to outpatient/home care-type services and, again, does not cover the full costs. This means that the experience of using healthcare for older American's requires an intimate knowledge of healthcare costs and an engagement with the healthcare market. Furthermore, some aspects of care, such as nursing homes, are explicitly excluded from coverage. We can examine the impact of this very different healthcare provision context on the expenditure and consumption patterns of older people. The Health and Retirement Survey (HRS) provides some insights, but differential reference periods and definitions render direct comparisons problematic. In the two years prior to the 2004 survey, 33% of those aged 65+ had been admitted to hospital (Karp, 2007) – an annual rate not dissimilar to that in the UK and showing a similar age-related increase from about 10% per annum for those aged 65-74 to 20% for those aged 85 and over. It is more problematic to make comparisons of other types of service use. HRS data indicate that approximately 95% of respondents consulted a doctor in the two years prior to the survey, but it is not clear what type of doctor was involved. We can demonstrate the effect of the availability of insurance on consumption of health services by examining the use of dentists by age. For those aged 55-64, almost 70% had been to a dentist in the previous two years compared with a little over 40% of those aged 85; dentistry is excluded from Medicare coverage. Overall, in terms of broad patterns of acute hospital use, there is a general similarity of utilisation between older people in the United States and Britain. This, perhaps, reflects the availability of basic health insurance to American older people. However, the non-comprehensive nature of the insurance is evident in the expenditure older Americans make in terms of healthcare and the impact this has on their expenditure budgets. Medicare insurance provides access to basic care (for example, shared rooms) and includes a contribution or co-payment by the older person. For example, a co-payment of $10 or $20 may be required for a consultation with a doctor (2007 data). We can see how this system affects the budgets of older people by using a variety of different datasets. Data from the

2005 US Consumer Expenditure Survey, the equivalent of the FES, reveal that those aged 65+ spend 13% of their annual income on out-of-pocket healthcare (this rises to 15.6% for those aged 75 and over). Of this, 3.7% of annual income for this age group is spent on drugs and 3% on medical services (www.bls. gov/cex/2005/share/age.pdf). This is an overall figure and clearly varies across the population. For those in the bottom quintile of the income distribution, direct healthcare-related payments may account for approximately 25% of their expenditure. HRS data indicate that out-of-pocket health expenditure increased from $1,450 per annum for those aged 55-64 to $2,200 for those aged 85+ (Karp, 2007). Again, these are almost certainly underestimates, as they do not include nursing home care and other health-related activities. The contrast between the UK and US is illustrated by the examination of health expenditure in the year before death. We have seen that in the UK this is the most 'expensive' phase of life in terms of healthcare costs. The same is true for the US, but there the direct effect on individuals is much greater. Karp (2007) reports longitudinal HRS data that estimate that for the average couple, health expenditure was approximately 15% of income five years before the death of a spouse, 25% on income three years before death and 50% in the final year of life. Private household spending on health may well be sensitive to changes in welfare spending. Meara and colleagues (2004) examined trends in health spending between 1963 and 2000 and found that spending accelerated over the period, increasing most rapidly among the elderly between 1963 and 1987. This trend reversed post-1987 and the authors attribute this to reforms to Medicaid. In the same period, prescription drug spending grew fastest among the non-elderly.

It is now part of established policy, at least in England, that people should either save or insure against elements of their health and social care needs (Deeming and Keen, 2003). This is a new and perhaps unexpected policy development. Parker and Clarke (1997) reported that most of the people they surveyed felt that the state should be the major provider of care to older people and that it has the ability to do so. They also found that the 18- to 64-year-olds studied were unable to estimate risks of needing care, or of requiring long-term care. Deeming and Keen (2002) also indicated that few contemporary pensioners had 'spare' income to pay for care.

Our analysis of expenditure surveys illustrates that while spending on direct healthcare remains relatively low among all age groups, including older people, spending on other areas, such as leisure and recreation, has increased. Income levels are related strongly to the capacity to apply household expenditure in these areas, but age of itself is not a necessary condition of low spending. We can only speculate as to how many of those older people currently paying for domiciliary care expected to have to do this in their old age and made provision for this expenditure. Here, we have the growth of health-related consumption that has arisen, in part at least, by the withdrawal of the state from the provision and/or funding of these services rather than through the 'positive' choice of older people. What we cannot determine is if these changes have improved the quality of provision received by older people.

Conclusion

This chapter has sought to explore the development of health-related consumption within the context of an NHS whereby the majority of older people use healthcare services that are free at the point of delivery. We have shown that we can trace health-related expenditure across the lifetime of the FES and that such expenditure has increased, although it is well below the levels reported for the United States. We have also been able to identify the emergence of expenditure patterns that reflect the development of health-related lifestyles, such as membership of gyms and leisure centres, and the involvement in leisure-related activities. As such, this is necessarily a very preliminary analysis and does not explore generational, class and gender differentials in these forms of consumption. These are issues that we believe merit further analysis, as does the broader topic of consumption and expenditure in later life.

EIGHT

Health and social policy: a moving target

Introduction

This chapter examines the evolution of consumerism in UK health and social welfare policy with particular respect to older people. The chapter outlines the chronology of changes in health and social policy that have particular resonance for older people and the significance of these changes within 'a society of consumers' (Bauman, 2007, p 52). We chart the development and expansion of the post-war welfare state from its origins in the late 1940s to the mid-1970s, the 'crisis' of the welfare state and the subsequent reformulation of welfare policy that took place during the 1980s and 1990s. We go on to outline the new conditions of welfare consumerism that have been pursued by new Labour within a 'choice and voice' agenda before addressing our final theme, the potential significance of devolution for the diversification of welfare policy in the new Britain of the 21st century. The chapter ends by considering the role of health and social policy in the reconstruction of the older citizen.

The development of health and social care for older people in the post-war period

Prior to the creation of the National Health Service (NHS) in July 1948, healthcare in Britain was provided by a mixed system of hospital and primary care provision that was generally regarded as inadequate and unfair. Hospital care varied by geographic area, depending in part on the strength of local voluntarism and on historical circumstance, and was unequal in terms of quality and quantity (Mohan, 2003). Access to acute hospital treatment and to what we now term primary care was mostly contingent on the ability to pay. Two parallel hospital systems existed: the voluntary sector, self-governing and independent, and public hospitals that were, in theory at least, under the control of the local authorities. Substantial proportions of the population were unable to afford care of any sort, while others had access to only rudimentary forms of healthcare. Among the most disenfranchised were older people and those with chronic conditions, physical and mental. Webster provides a vivid portrait of their plight:

> The vast majority [of older people] had lost all of their teeth, usually
> early in maturity. Those in need of glasses relied on the services of

Woolworth's…. The elderly became deaf without access to hearing aids and they lost their mobility without expectation of remedial assistance…. When the doctor was unavoidable they accepted with stoicism second class treatment in crowded surgeries or crippling fees occasioned by domiciliary visits…. Effective treatment was inaccessible while consultant services and advanced medical treatment were restricted to large medical centres…. Their health was poor and their expectations low. (Webster, 1991, pp 167–8)

Such was the position of older people when the 1946 National Health Service Act and the 1948 National Assistance Act were passed, promising to 'open a new and happier chapter for the old, the infirm … and others in need' (Ministry of Health 1949 report, cited by Webster, 1991, p165). Under the NHS, a system of free universal healthcare was to be established, the old poor law infirmaries and lunatic asylums closed or integrated with acute and specialist hospitals under regional hospital boards and provision made for home nursing services delivered under the auspices of local health authorities. Social care needs were to be addressed by local authorities primarily through residential care services, but in 'homes' where they would be treated more as honoured guests than workhouse inmates. An amending Act to the 1946 National Assistance Act was passed in 1962 that introduced the idea of 'community care' by requiring local authorities to provide welfare services for people aged 65 and over *in their own home* (Bell, 1965).

From its inception, the post-war welfare state struggled with distinguishing health needs from social needs, much as the poor law had done in assigning indoor and outdoor relief to older people. With the introduction of a National Health Service, this boundary became more salient and more contested throughout the period. Confusion arising from the ambiguous wording of the two formative Acts led to concerns being raised at the time that frail older people may fall between the two forms of provision. Governments responded initially by expanding and segmenting local authority residential care, creating a distinction between those needing 'residential' care for primarily social reasons and those requiring 'specialist' provision, such as residential homes for 'the elderly mentally infirm' based on their 'special needs'. Meanwhile, many of the institutional provisions of the poor law infirmaries had been converted into specialist long-term geriatric and psychogeriatric hospital wards, turning residents into patients and patients into residents, as the nature of need was constantly redefined across the two institutional sectors (Sinclair, 1988).

Throughout the 1950s and 1960s, the care typically provided for older people remained primarily institutional and the number of chronic long-stay beds – in geriatric and mental hospitals – rose steadily, as did the number of local authority residential home places. Community provision remained limited. Then, from the 1970s onwards, there was a shift towards addressing the 'community needs' of 'old people at home'. The over-65s had been a minority of the recipients of these services in the 1940s and 1950s, but during the 1960s and 1970s, the work of home helps and home nurses gradually focused on the needs of people over 65. Even so, as late as 1970, the indicative level for the provision of home nursing was limited to one nurse per thousand and for home care 12 home helps per thousand people aged 65 and over. Free prescriptions, free eyesight tests and glasses and free false teeth had been widely welcomed by older people when the NHS was introduced, but these free goods lasted for a few idealistic years before charges were introduced – with initially no exceptions made for those over 65 years old.

The costs of institutional care – personal, social and financial – became more apparent and a new focus emerged on 'rehabilitation' and the need to expand provision of continuing care in the community (Millard and Higgs, 1989). Numerous reports highlighted the 'harm' produced by 'inappropriate' institutional care and the creation of 'unnecessary' dependency and excess disabilities (Townsend, 1981; Booth et al, 1983). Attempts were made to 'plan' the appropriate balance of provision – of hospital and residential care beds, of day-care places and of community services through various forms of 'inter-agency' collaboration between health and local authorities. The shift towards reduced hospital bed use and improved community care and the better coordination of health and social care meant to be brought about by this joint care planning failed to usher in the hoped for new 'golden age' for domiciliary services' (Means, 1986, p 104). Although there was some evidence that joint finance schemes helped ease the problem of 'bed blocking', it was apparent that this centrally driven programme was failing to exercise the leverage required to transform the delivery of health and social care for older, vulnerable people (Ferlie et al, 1985).

Meanwhile, the fiscal crisis of the state in the late 1970s made the need to find alternative sources of leverage more acute. Change had proved hard to bring about; there was still a heavy emphasis on local authority and NHS long-stay beds, and a correspondingly limited system of community care. At this point, there was a change in government and with it a change of approach to health and social care policy. Britain's new conservative government began to dissolve the post-war consensus that had been built up around the Keynesian welfare state. Controversial as this break was at the time, as Higgs has pointed out, public expenditure was already seen by theorists of both the left and right as a major cause of economic recession within the world economy. Welfare spending was seen as central to the economic crisis facing the nation, because it was deemed both 'unproductive' and 'inefficient' (Higgs, 1993, p 20). In order to resolve this crisis, a neoconservative (later transformed into a neoliberal) agenda was fashioned, aimed at introducing a market discipline into all aspects of welfare, while targeting those most in need.

The transformation of welfare

In 1983, Margaret Thatcher's Conservative government was re-elected with a much-expanded parliamentary majority. During the first period in government, change had been made hesitantly. Now the government saw itself in a stronger political position and it began to implement a sustained programme of reducing public expenditure at the same time as relaunching the move towards community care. The closure of NHS long-stay hospital beds was helped by the ability of a wider population to access 'funded' nursing home beds as a result of changes introduced in means-tested supplementary benefits (income support). The consequences of this change in benefits (which meant that people without sufficient means could use their income support to pay for their private nursing home care) led to the expansion of nursing home provision, sparking debate over what appeared to be an uncontrolled transformation in health and social long-term care provision (Baldwin and Corden, 1987). But as more people were able to 'purchase' long-stay nursing home care, it became easier to close long-stay NHS beds and to represent older people as 'consumers' choosing their long-term care rather than as geriatric or psychogeriatric patients assigned to a long-stay bed, by the intervention of third parties (Willcocks et al, 1987, p 38). Just how large this redistribution of funds to 'privately purchased' long-stay beds was can be seen by the fact that, within just 10 years, from 1980 to 1990, payments to people in independent residential and nursing homes rose from £10 million to over £1,270 million (Darton and Wright, 1992).

The leverage introduced to foster such marketisation of health and social care was the 'new managerialism' that sought a much more accountable and business like approach to purchasing and providing care (Davies, 1987; Hood, 1991, 1995). This approach was exemplified by the work of the Audit Commission, which produced two key reports in the mid-1980s, called *Managing social services for the elderly more effectively* and *Making a reality of community care* (Audit Commission, 1985, 1986). These reports identified what the Commission saw as significant 'inefficiencies' in the organisation of, and inter-relationships between, community and institutional provision of services for frail elderly people. According to the Commission, services were characterised by poor lines of accountability, fragmentation and poor levels of cooperation and coordination, and the inefficient allocation of resources.

The government responded by first funding a review of community services under Sir Roy Griffiths culminating in the Griffiths report (Griffiths, 1988) and, a year later, introducing a White Paper, *Caring for people* (DH, 1989) that paved the way for subsequent legislation in the form of the 1990 NHS and Community Care Act (DH, 1990). The Act marked a dramatic change in policy, introducing a clear separation between those agencies providing care and those responsible for purchasing or commissioning it. Health authorities were to 'commission' healthcare on behalf of their local population, including care provided in NHS or equivalent private nursing home long-stay beds, using funds delegated to them on the basis of capitation. Local authority social services, meanwhile, would commission social care packages based on the formal assessment of clients' needs. In effect, health and local authorities became proxy purchasers of care on behalf of older and vulnerable people, while hospitals and nursing homes became commissioned providers, whose performance in delivering efficient 'customer care' was to be carefully monitored by the purchasing organisations.

The NHS and Community Care Act was followed by a flurry of circulars and letters specifying guidance and recommending principles of good practice. The rhetoric referred to the need for a 'seamless service', 'agency agreements' and 'shared values'. While internal markets threatened to fragment services, the focus in these circulars was on key areas of joint working, such as hospital discharge planning and arrangements for continuing care. At the same time, the consumer citizen model was further promoted through such schemes as the Patient's Charter (1991), which was presented as a means of maintaining quality and standards of care in the NHS by informing users of healthcare services what they as customers could expect. In 1992, an amendment to the 1948 National Assistance Act (Choice of Accommodation Direction) was introduced, designed to 'ensure that when councils with social services responsibilities make placements in care homes or care homes providing nursing care that, within reason, individuals are able to exercise genuine choice over where they live' (Secretary of State for Health, 1992). This was followed, in 1996, by further new legislation (1996 Community Care (Direct Payments) Act) enabling local authorities to give cash payments to individuals needing services in order that they, the clients, could 'secure for themselves' the services they needed (DH, 2000b).

Obtaining services in the 1990s was increasingly spoken of as 'shopping' for care, as the reforms of the 1990s introduced and institutionalised (quasi-) markets into health and social care. There followed further privatisation of significant elements of long-stay NHS provision for frail older people and the progressive de-institutionalisation of community care provision into a diversity of private care agencies. Although some aspects of this market rhetoric of customer care and consumer choice would prove difficult to implement, because of established professional practice, the lack or limited number of competitor organisations, the practical difficulties of shifting resources and the constraints on consumer knowledge and behaviour, the consequences were real enough – in terms of radically changing the balance of provision of institutional and community social welfare from the statutory to the independent sector.

Another consequence of this 'marketisation' was the growth of 'consumerist advocacy' services, acting as the voice of those newly rebranded as 'customers', 'clients' or 'users' of health and social care. The rhetoric of consumerism and customer care merged easily with that of the identity politics of the 1960s and 1970s, as they were gradually incorporated into the philosophy of the 'new-style' voluntary sector. Organisations sought political and social 'accreditation' as the representatives of particular groups of 'users' and 'carers'. Increasingly, these voices were invited to play the part of 'proxy consumers' in this new 'quasi-market' welfare discourse. These new consumer citizens were no longer confined to representing the sick and the infirm. Following the passage of the Carers (Recognition and Services) Act in 1995, the families of people needing 'care' were recognised as equally legitimate voices and entitled recipients of rebadged 'carer' services (DH 1995). Although the problems facing carers of sick and disabled family members had been widely recognised during the 1980s (Charlesworth et al, 1984; Parker, 1990; Social Services Committee 1990), after the passing of this Act, caring and carer became formally recognised categories. Relatives now had the right to demand that their needs, as well as those of their 'dependants', be assessed and (*ceteris paribus*) met. The Act created a new market and new and rather more vociferous consumers.

Organisations representing users and/or carers, such as Age Concern (established in 1971), the Alzheimer's Disease Society (now Alzheimer's Society) (established in 1979), Carers UK (established in 1988), Counsel and Care (established in 1974), the Disabled Living Foundation (established in 1973) and the United Kingdom's Disabled People's Council (established in 1981), grew in size and influence, stimulated by, and in turn stimulating, the consumerist turn in health and social care (Potter, 1988). In the process, these advocacy organisations became gradually more market-oriented in their search for funds, members and lobbying power. Success breeds success and it soon became an implicit requirement, both centrally and locally, for the commissioners of health and social care actively to seek representatives from such organisations to join the various bodies charged with planning and purchasing services for frail elderly people and their carers.

Modernisation and the market: citizens and consumers under New Labour

When the Conservatives were defeated in 1997, the new Labour government that succeeded them pursued a similar strategy in its health and social care policies. Claiming that it was 'modernising' rather than marketising a new style NHS – for example, *The new NHS: Modern, dependable* (DH, 1997), *Saving lives: Our healthier nation* (DH, 1999) and *The NHS plan* (DH, 2000a) – it expanded the 'consumer rights' approach that had been developed by the various citizen charters of the previous Conservative government. As part of this 'modernisation', the new Labour government set up the National Institute for Clinical Excellence and produced a series of National Service Frameworks designed to lay out the kinds and qualities of services that various 'patient' groups should expect to receive (although by this time, these new initiatives were targeted for guidance and implementation in England, devolution resulting in differences from, or delays in, following what had now become English rather than UK health and social care policy). The National Service Framework (NSF) for older people in England (DH, 2003) was one of the first to come out. Its aims reflected a strategy based on 'voice and choice'. The first 'standard' was to prevent discrimination on the grounds of age in the provision of healthcare services, followed by other 'standards' aimed at reducing disability and the need for long-term care, maximising independent living and enhancing the well-being of older people and their carers. User and carer representatives were expected to contribute as partners in implementing the NSF and partnership bodies, typically drawing from local branch organisations of the larger national charities such as Age Concern, the Alzheimer's Society, MIND (the National Association of Mental Health, representing elderly mentally frail people) and Carers UK, set up to monitor and report on progress.

New Labour consolidated the consumerisation of health and social care in a number of ways. First, it oversaw the continuing expansion of independent provision of long-term care places and community/home care, effectively removing NHS institutional provision in England to the very margins. Second, it encouraged the involvement of advocacy organisations both as 'consumer' representatives and as 'providers' in the mixed economy of care. Third, it promoted 'direct payments' enabling older people to buy in the services they needed, and finally, it emphasised the importance of health promotion and disease prevention, encouraging individuals to look after their own health and well-being throughout life. During the 1980s, the number of older people who lived in a residential home for social or economic reasons, rather than for reasons of infirmity, had begun to decline significantly. In 1970, most of the over 65-year-olds living in institutional long-stay care were residents of local authority-run homes. Most of the residents of these homes were able to walk, dress, feed and generally look after themselves without much help. By 1980, the number of people who needed looking after had increased but still at least half of the residents in old people's homes were fairly independent (Booth et al, 1983; Bebbington and Tong, 1986; Willcocks et al, 1987). By 1990, the majority of those living in residential or nursing homes were no longer independent, and the dominant form of long-stay institutional care had shifted decisively from the old people's home to the nursing home (Victor, 1992). A particularly detailed account of this transition was made by Chris Smith in Nottinghamshire, where places in private nursing homes were virtually non-existent in 1979, but by the end of the 1980s, exceeded the number of places in local authority residential care (Smith, 1992).

Thus, the intensification of institutional dependency was accompanied by the move from statutory to private provision, itself triggered by the changes to the rules for supplementary benefits in 1983. A similar shift – towards greater levels of dependency among those older people receiving care and increased provision of community care by the independent sector – was slower to take off. Although the post-1993 implementation of the social care elements of the 1990 NHS and Community Care Act increased the amount of care provided by the independent sector, it was during the period of New Labour that this trend towards independent provision really took off, as Figure 8.1 shows.

More than two thirds of the recorded provision of home care is delivered to 'clients' aged 75 and over (The Information Centre 2007: www.ic.nhs.uk) and by 2000 the majority of such care was provided by independent agencies. By 2006, over three quarters of community social care was being provided by the independent sector. Levels of provision have narrowed and intensified. In 1997, 1,389 contact

Figure 8.1: Proportion of home care contacts provided by statutory versus independent service providers, 1997-2006

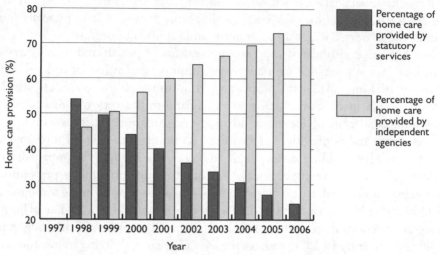

Source: www.ic.nhs.uk

home care hours were recorded per 10,000 households, which were received by 238 households per 10,000; by 2006, the amount of home care had increased to 1,828 hours but it was received by fewer households – 169 households per 10,000 (ONS/DH 2002, 2004; ONS/NHS 2006, 2007).

If the shift to independent providers reflects the marketisation of social care, its narrowing and intensification reflects the new managerialism. Whether this 'improved' vertical targeting of resources facilitates greater independence remains unclear. Are those unable to access socially funded home care because their needs are too few to warrant it now purchasing care for themselves or are they simply doing without? If the latter, is the consequence greater personal vulnerability or are people spurred to greater independence by having to do more for themselves? Has the increased intensity of provision enabled more people to remain at home who would otherwise be offered a long-stay bed in their choice of a care home? Whether the market and the new managerialism is empowering or enfeebling older people remains to be seen.

In the 1960s and 1970s, when plans were developed to build new residential homes for old people or purpose-built 'geriatric' and 'psychogeriatric' units for the long-term care of frail elderly people, those advising on their design were largely professionals – architects, senior social services personnel, civil servants and academics, as well as representatives from those charitable bodies who were themselves providers of long-term care in the small voluntary sector. Community consultation was unheard of and the only advocates the future residents and patients would have would be their family. By the 1980s, new voices were emerging, not only from the private nursing home and residential industry, but also from national bodies such as the National Consumer Council and the National Council forVoluntary Organisations (Potter, 1988, p 152).Advocacy bodies such as Age Concern, the Alzheimer's Society, Counsel and Care, the Carers National Association (now Carer's UK), the Independent Living Foundation and MIND were increasing their membership, while developing a more professional approach to advancing their influence on policy.

As their role in advocacy grew, so did their membership and their command of financial resources. When the Alzheimer's Society was established in 1979, it had no more than a few local branches, a turnover of less than a quarter of a million pounds, and a membership in the hundreds. Some 30 years later, its membership stands at around 25,000, its annual income is over £37 million and it has over 260 local branches across England and Wales. Organisations such as Age Concern, Carers UK and Counsel and Care have benefited equally from the fertile ground of the new consumerism in health and social care.They have all seen their membership, finances and influence grow, as they have become key 'stakeholders' in the mixed economy of care that characterises Britain in the 21st century.

The evolution of community services under new Labour has also witnessed the rise of individualised 'purchaser' power, in the form of 'direct payments' to frail and infirm older people. This 'right' enabling disabled people to exercise greater choice over the kinds of care they receive and the kinds of providers from whom they receive care was first established for disabled people of working age. It was extended to people aged 65 and over in 1996, through the Community Care (Direct Payments) Act, passed in the final year of John Major's Conservative government (DH, 1996).The right of older people to receive direct payments to purchase care for themselves is illustrative of a broader, international trend in the consumerisation of welfare policy. Increasingly, governments across a wide range of welfare system regimes are passing legislation devolving purchasing power and the choice and control that accompanies such power to those individuals who are most in need of care and assistance (Timonen et al, 2006).

Britain's New Labour government has put considerable pressure on local authorities to expand their direct payments schemes and has established the Direct Payments Development Fund to facilitate its implementation. Direct service provision – the model of personal home care that was established by the NHS and National Assistance Acts and that took off substantially during the 1970s and 1980s – is seen now as inflexible, unresponsive, inefficient and overly paternalistic. Direct payments offer consumer choice and consumer power and, by carefully controlling eligibility criteria, direct payments are also seen as potentially cheaper. Department of Health policy guidelines suggest that '[b]y employing innovative and creative options, it may be possible for users to identify alternatives (to existing services) which both cost less and meet their needs effectively' (DH, 2000b, p 18).

Increasing the number of people over retirement age who purchase their own care is difficult to achieve, however, when the new managerialism also requires greater vertical targeting. As the criteria for neediness have risen steadily, the capacity of those entitled to receive direct payments to behave as informed purchasers of care has declined. Figure 8.2 below indicates just how small are the numbers of older people who are receiving direct payments and just how limited their progressive implementation has been within this age group. Transforming the heaviest consumers of welfare into its principal purchasers is an uphill task. It is, however, one of huge iconic significance if the citizen–consumer approach is to thrive.

If the costs of long-term care are to be managed, as well as the standards of care improved, it may not be enough to introduce competition among providers, promote the third sector's role as 'stakeholders' and devolve purchasing power to those who most need care and support. The criteria for eligibility cannot be endlessly raised; 'neediness' itself must be reduced. The prospect of more people living well beyond the 'traditional' three score years and 10 seems to require more effort spent on the promotion and maintenance of 'well-being' throughout life. This new need – for people to learn do-it-yourself health maintenance – has been central to New Labour's public health agenda, epitomised by the Department of Health report *Our health, our care, our say: A new direction for community services* (DH, 2006). This report, phrased appropriately enough in the consumerist mode of choice and voice, places a new emphasis on health promotion and the prevention of disease and disability, with more active systems of screening and the implementation of models for the self-management of disease, and improved community social care services to prevent hospital admissions. In the absence of evidence that particular preventative strategies do reduce the need for care in later life, the report proposes Partnerships for Older People Projects (POPPs) in order

Figure 8.2: Proportion of clients receiving community care as 'direct payments', by age group (England)

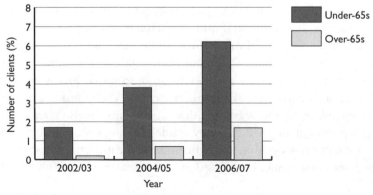

Source: www.ic.nhs.uk

to gather evidence for what helps promote well-being and prevent ill health and disability in later life. Future consumers are also expected to be 'self-employed' managers of disease as well as 'self-promoters' of well-being.

Devolution and diversification in policy

Thus far, we have concentrated on trends in health and social care policy since the inception of the post-war welfare state in the late 1940s. Half a century on, the trajectory of Britain's welfare state looks as if it may start following more diverse paths, reflecting the diversity of Europe as a whole. This is the result of the devolution of government, which has created the Scottish Parliament and the Welsh Assembly, each of which have begun to implement their own distinct versions of welfare reform. Significant differences among the three nations are already evident, most notably in regard to policy for the care of frail elderly people. In this final section of the chapter, we consider the implications of this new diversity in citizenship for the future of ageing.

One of the more important policy differences has been the funding of free personal and nursing care for older people in Scotland. This diversification in national policies arose out of a number of factors, but was triggered by the different responses made by the major political parties in Westminster and Edinburgh to the UK government-appointed Royal Commission on Long Term Care. The Commission's report (Royal Commission on Long Term Care, 1999) condemned the haphazard and piecemeal nature of long-term care, the ways in which individuals were lost in and overwhelmed by the system and the ambiguities that surrounded groups of patients who were both 'too well' to be cared for by the NHS, yet 'too sick' to be cared for in residential settings. The Commission made a number of recommendations to address these shortcomings, the most important being that the government should make personal and nursing care free to all. In its response, the UK government accepted most of the recommendations but rejected the key one of providing free personal care, choosing instead to provide free NHS nursing care and charge for personal care as meeting 'social' not 'health' needs (DH, 2000b). This effectively meant that older people in England and Wales contributed, depending on their means, to the costs of their accommodation and personal care in residential or nursing care homes, while their age peers in Scotland, under the 2002 Community Care and Health (Scotland) Act, had their personal care paid for by their local authority, irrespective of their means, although still contributing to the costs of their 'board and lodging'. In England, the 2001 Health and Social Care Act formalised the arrangements for paying for long-term care by the use of the Registered Nursing Care Contribution tool. This instrument was designed to formally assess the amount of registered nursing care needed, which would be categorised on the basis of bandings (high, medium and low), with 'high' meriting completely free NHS care and 'low' meriting none beyond that available through existing primary healthcare services. The divergent responses to the

Royal Commission between the UK New Labour government and the Scottish Parliament (where New Labour also formed the administration) can perhaps better be understood in terms of competing forms of citizenship rather than as a result of differential responses to consumer-led advocacy. Devolution was, after all, New Labour policy, and it was important that the New Labour administration be seen to be adequately representing its Scottish constituents. The Scottish Nationalist Party (SNP) saw free personal care for older people as a key point of distinction between English and Scottish policy and hence a marker of competing models of citizenship, one giving 'universal' rights, the other 'conditional rights'. The SNP successfully campaigned for implementing in full the recommendations of Lord Sutherland's Royal Commission, forcing the New Labour-led Scottish government to break ranks with its Westminster colleagues and pass the 2002 Act (Marnoch, 2003). The new Welsh Assembly also chose to make its mark in policy diversification, initially focusing its efforts on issues to do with language and education (Scourfield et al, 2008). Subsequently, encouraged no doubt by the example of New Labour in Scotland, the Assembly has turned its attention to its senior citizens and in 2003 the Assembly produced its first-ever Strategy for Older People in Wales (WAG, 2003). Unlike the devolutionary focus on 'free personal care' in Scotland, the new Welsh government espoused a more dynamic approach in its strategy, emphasising instead a 'programme of citizenship' to support older people. This is based on the need to combat ageism, tackle stereotypes of old age, encourage economic and social participation, promote good health, prevent ill health and 'promote a confident flexible and viable care home sector' when promotion and prevention fail (WAG, 2003). Following on from the strategy, the Assembly established the post of Commissioner for Older People, an independent figure with a remit to ensure that the voice of older people is heard at a local and national level. This development was promoted by New Labour's First Minister as 'breaking new ground anywhere in the world' (BBC News, 2008). This close focus on later life has not, however, resulted in any major policy differences from the central government in Westminster. The NSF for older people in Wales (WAG, 2006) contains essentially the same agenda as the earlier English version published in 2001, and it remains to be seen if the agenda for older people has had any measurable impact on the lives of Wales' senior citizens.

Devolution may yet bring its own set of problems, as Northern Ireland, Scotland and Wales all face large sunk costs in services needing modernisation with local vested interests attempting to maintain the status quo (Greer, 2004). Devolution may add further to the fragmentation of services to older people and to further tensions between the goals of universal provision and local needs. Overall, devolution may not have had any distinct impact on the performance of personal social and health care services (Andrews and Martin, 2007). Nevertheless, what has emerged from the devolution of central government in the UK is the recreation of a citizenship agenda, in Scotland and Wales, echoing that of the post-war era. How distinct this agenda will be from that of the more generic citizen consumer is impossible to tell. What it does suggest is that the 'choice and voice' agenda is itself capable of leading policy in different directions at once.

The significance of the consumerist approach to health and welfare for the reconstruction of later life

Patient choice has been one of the main drivers behind New Labour's consumerist project (Clarke et al, 2005; McDonald, 2006). Drawing on the work and advice of Le Grand (2003), the government sees the promotion of choice and consumerist behaviour as a means to deliver quality improvements and make services more responsive to needs, while at the same time challenging professional interests and holding down costs through increasing competition among service providers. Those who see benefits in competition and choice emphasise that competition within the reformed system will be based on quality not price. The benefits envisaged include a greater range of services for individuals to consider and competition by providers on the basis of quality, it is argued, will help drive up quality of services. However, the evidence that this is happening is limited and improvements where they occur are not necessarily the result of increased choice (Appleby et al, 2003). Those most able to exercise choice choose by and large to stay away from social services, establishing their own forms of support through family relationships and the exchange of favours between friends and neighbours. The majority of older people may well end up making direct payments, but not through local authority-administered schemes. Rather, they will choose to pay for the help they need through buying in the services of carers, cleaners and gardeners, if and when there are no others in the house who can help.

In a current estimated population made up of some 8.7 million people aged 65 years and above, 1.2 million (14%) were, in 2006/07, recipients (users) of some type of funded service mediated by local authorities. For over a million (over 80%), this was a service delivered to their home, to enable them to continue living at home. Of those one million 'users', only 17,000 (0.2% of the 65+ population) were receiving direct payments. Given these figures, it is important to understand that for older people engagement with consumer culture is not now, nor is it likely ever to be, mediated significantly by structure and organisation of personal community services.

Despite the marginality of social care for the day-to-day lives of most older people, the discourse in which policy and practice towards older groups in society is embedded now draws on the concept of 'active ageing' and the consumerism inherent in such framing of later life. Active ageing evolved as a term from earlier conceptualisations of 'productive ageing' and 'positive ageing' that have their roots in the US and its consumerist, commercialised culture. Like much American culture, it has a strong influence. The World Health Organization (WHO) has emphasised active ageing in its work (WHO, 2002) and defines it in terms of enabling individuals to participate in society within a capabilities framework (Sen, 1985).

In the UK, these ideas have driven the development of policies in health, social care and welfare (DH, 2005), although not without voices expressing unease. Walker (2006) has identified what he considers to be a number of flaws in this approach. These include the strong rhetorical flavour of these policies (at the expense of concrete interventions), which has led to a shift in responsibility from the state to the individual; an emphasis on employment and labour market participation rather than universal citizenship; and an almost exclusive focus on the frail, dependent and 'oldest' old. Although these policies are directed towards vulnerable groups, older vulnerable people themselves have had limited input into the formation of policy – in contrast to advocacy groups, which clearly have had considerable influence, at least in shaping the discourse of policy, and for which activity and agency are of supreme significance in their role as advocates.

The fiscal crisis of the welfare state, the expansion of identity politics into the arena of health and welfare, the rise of consumerism and the construction of the consumerist voice, as well as the very real material improvement in the health and well-being of the older population, have combined to make 'active ageing' a dominant paradigm for health and social policy. Its emphases on autonomy, choice and consumer rights reflect processes that privilege agency, autonomy, individualisation and personal responsibility, while underscoring the need to limit collective provision to those who are least able to look after themselves. Such people are also the least able, mentally and physically, to represent themselves as other than personally as well as structurally dependent. But despite their lack of a voice – individual or otherwise – other bodies have emerged to advocate and act on their collective behalf, retaining the idea of agency through the practice of consumer advocacy and the politics of identity – the choice and voice agenda of the 21st century.

Health and social policies deliver care in a more commodified, and also more individualised, form than was the case during the development of the post-war welfare state. This change in policy reflects more than shapes contemporary culture. But it also creates new tensions, not least between the desire to support individual decision making and the need effectively to target collective resources. In November 2007, the Commission for Social Care Inspection found that 73% of local authorities were planning to refuse care to everyone whose needs were not considered to be 'substantial' (Carvel, 2007). In December of the same year, the UK government announced plans to transform the organisation of social care in England and Wales (DH 2007), giving direct control to older people over how and where money will be spent with the introduction of personal budgets for everyone eligible for adult social care. While these proposals will effectively turn social care into a consumer expenditure item, as eligibility criteria are shifted further towards those in greatest need, the gap between the rhetoric of choice and the reality of need can only widen. Those most entitled to purchase their own care will be least able to go 'shopping' – whatever the nature of goods and services on offer. This gap between economic empowerment and personal neediness provides opportunities for new agents to emerge, advocates, interpreters and quasi-independent brokers speaking on behalf of those too frail to voice their needs (Gilleard and Higgs, 1998). The growing impetus to promote consumerism in welfare will see such players continue to grow in significance, just as the proportion of older people entitled to access community care will continue to shrink.

Conclusion

Social and health policy with respect to older people is facing a moving target, as new cohorts enter later life with different expectations from those held by older people who had reached adult life when the institutions of the post-war welfare state were developing. The transformation of welfare policies during the 1980s is central to those changing expectations. The new individualism seems set to continue to evolve. The Wanless report into social care for older people (Wanless, 2006) has already pointed out that the rising expectations of the baby boomers will be one of the most pressing concerns for policy makers in the next few decades. These changes in expectations reflect new ways of thinking about public services in an era of increasingly individualised citizen consumership (see Greener, 2008 for a discussion of the various modalities of the term). There is continuous pressure to move away from welfare forms that emphasise universal social protection, decommodification and unconditional benefits, to forms that focus rather on social inclusion, commodification, consultation and conditionally targeted benefit systems (Gilbert, 2002). In part, this reflects the shift towards 'productivism' within welfare policy (European Commission, 2000; Lewis, 2007) with its focus on participation in the labour market. Not only does this potentially exacerbate gender inequality in later life as well as cause difficulties in terms of intergenerational transfers (Kotlikoff, 2003), but it also shifts attention away from older citizens' entitlements and towards family units with children (Esping-Andersen, 2002). However, it may also correspond with a move away from viewing later life mainly as a category of need and towards one that fits more comfortably with the individualising aspects of consumer society, even if that sometimes means viewing older people through the prism of disability rights and proxy consumerism.

The theme of this book is the rise of consumerism and the increasing engagement of older people with consumer society. The growth of consumerism in health and social care policies and the refocusing on 'customer care' reflects this more general cultural shift and the deconstruction of the relationship between citizen and the state that the post-war welfare regimes had reconstructed. That relationship may have emphasised universal social rights, but it did so at a time when the conditions of life for most older people were mean and meagre and universal long-term care existed largely within the framework of the surviving institutions of public assistance and the poor law. For those inclined to sentimentalise the 'old' welfare state, it is salutary to record the reports of institutional abuse in the 1960s and 1970s, the de-individualising regimes of the NHS long-stay hospitals, the readiness to offer institutional care in the absence of community support, the limited provision of personal care that was available in the community and the institutionalised regimes of the day hospitals and day centres of that time (Bennett, 1999).

Whatever the claims of 'universal' care, the reality of those decades, from the 1950s to the 1970s, was that much remained unchanged. There was still marked variation in levels of home and institutional care, central targets for the provision of care were rarely heeded and, as now, most personal care provided to older people was provided by other older people. What has changed is the narrowing of the client population seen as eligible for 'care' and the rise in the proportion of people whose age no longer qualifies them as 'deserving' of welfare. Meanwhile, lives continue to get longer, just as the number of people employed in the private and public health and social care sectors expands. There is little reason to believe that the divide between private and public provision has any significant impact on either service effectiveness or cost efficiency (Andersen and Blegvad, 2006) and the debate often concerns the economic costs and benefits for staff rather than the relative costs and benefits to the recipients of care. Whether the relentless rhetoric of consumerism will eventually lead to a change in the reality of care may depend less on policy and more on present and future generational change in the habitus of welfare.

The devolution of health and social care policy to national parliaments represents a different type of opportunity to explore the impact of diversification on conceptualisations of later life and older people. Time will tell whether such diversification acts as a driver to improve the position of older people or whether it simply refashions the old rhetoric of care in a new national garb. Since the crisis of the welfare state, national policies have chosen to ape the rhetoric of the market, speaking of clients, consumers and customers rather than patients, residents and citizens (Potter, 1988; Needham, 2006). While these policies of choice and voice, of active ageing and consumer citizenship may suit the desires and aspirations of many of those reaching retirement age in the 21st century, in all the countries that make up the United Kingdom, the greater challenge remains to adapt them to the reality of those who otherwise end up living their old age within other people's rules. Whether the opportunities of devolution for promoting active senior citizenship or the global progress in promoting citizen consumership can best change that experience remains to be seen.

NINE

Conclusion

Introduction

In this book we have traced a growing engagement with consumer society among the older age groups over the last 40 years of the 20th century. While this engagement has been both varied and uneven, the overall trend has been one of increasing ownership of and expenditure on key consumer goods during this period (from a low baseline). These changes in the consumption patterns of the older population reflect other deep and lasting transformations in British society that have left their mark on the landscape of British social, economic and political life. These include the long-term decline of mass employment in manufacturing industries, changes in educational achievement and occupational mobility patterns, changes in gender relations and a freeing up of the public and private spheres. We have suggested that it is in the context of a shift towards late modernity that we are best able to understand the implications of these transformations for later life. The trends of increasing heterogeneity within the older population and the latter's increasing similarity with the general population have profound consequences for the experience of ageing in late modern society. In particular, the conditions of late modernity have given rise to increasing individualisation and a late modern sensibility based around the construction of individual identities through the pursuit and maintenance of lifestyles. These lifestyles are themselves increasingly commodified and framed by a consumer culture. In terms of levels of income and expenditure, therefore, it would appear that older people in Britain are not dissimilar in their profiles and habits to the rest of the population. Hence, these trends have a wider resonance within the study of ageing and later life. In this concluding chapter, we focus on the connections between lifestyles and consumption in later life in three important respects: first, a third age based on generational habitus; second, the contradictions of later life in consumer capitalism; and third, worlds of welfare and the 'consumer citizen'.

The third age and generational habitus

In the opening chapters of the book, we chartered the social and economic changes that occurred in the latter decades of the 20th century. In so doing, we highlighted the importance of period, cohort and generation for understanding later life. Previous work on generations has been hampered by confusion surrounding the term. In response, we utilised Gilleard and Higgs' (2005) theoretical approach to generations, which used Bourdieu's concepts of 'habitus' and 'field' to redefine Mannheim's concept of generational location as a cultural field and redefined generational consciousness as a generational habitus. Generation, following on from this, is therefore better understood as a cultural field that forms and is formed by particular tastes and dispositions. In the context of late modernity, these are the tastes and dispositions of those cohorts whose life worlds have been influenced by mass culture. Furthermore, in viewing generational consciousness as 'habitus', that is, as a set of structured and structuring dispositions that fashion individual practices, generational habitus can serve as a source of social power and as a basis for social differentiation and distinction. This alternative reading of generation allows us to move away from a 'thin' view of generation as a cohort that has experienced particular socialising events towards a 'thicker' understanding of generation as a temporally located cultural field within which individuals, from a variety of overlapping birth cohorts, participate as generational agents. Viewing later life through the prism of generational habitus has a number of advantages. It avoids the conflation between age groups, cohorts and periods that is common to generational thinking. In addition, agency is accounted for by defining a generational field according to the pattern of linkages between individual lifestyle practices. At the same time, the material conditions that structure patterns and linkages of engagement are recognised, thus allowing a better understanding of the mechanisms that drive the circuits of cultural capital. Drawing on this formulation of generational habits, we suggest that it is possible to consider the third age, in late modernity, as a cultural field where later life becomes more diverse and heterogeneous. Within the context of a post-scarcity westernised lifecourse, it is no longer appropriate to categorise people entering later life as a homogenous group of 'retirees', 'third-agers' or indeed 'pensioners'. Instead, post-working life is based around a variety of lifestyles, uncertainties, anxieties and aspirations. Furthermore, the cultural field that comprises the 'third age' transcends social distinctions based around age, class, status, race or gender. The crucial underpinning to this cultural field is the rise of mass consumer society and the post-war changes in the nature of globalised capitalism as well as the transformation of consumption practices that successive generations take with them into later life. In this sense, the sustainability of the third age as a cultural field is dependent on the material conditions of expanding global commodity capitalism and its associated consumer culture.

The contradictions of later life in consumer capitalism

The arguments and evidence set out in this book emphasise the important role of the emergence of consumer society in changing the nature of later life during the closing decades of the 20th century. At the same time, we have shown that patterns of consumption in later life reflect the uneven nature of retirement. There are limits to the analyses undertaken in this volume and because of the constraints of the data care must be taken when making interpretations. However, there is sufficient evidence to demonstrate the need for further detailed work to be undertaken on patterns of consumption among older groups and the importance of consumption in the construction of later life. There is now a large body of work stressing the importance of processes of consumption in the formation of social identities, but much of the research in this area has focused on younger age groups. It is unsustainable to assume that older people, simply by virtue of being old, are somehow immune to, or excluded from, the dynamics of consumer society. In fact, as we have tried to argue in this book, the cohorts of people retiring today are bound up in those processes that led to the growth of a post-war consumer culture. Their generational habitus developed with the emergence of youth-orientated consumer markets that were purposefully aimed at sub-cultures within cohorts of young people with newly acquired levels of disposable income. A generational field was built up around practices of consumption that provided the basis for the construction of individualised lifestyles and cultural identities. These practices, the continuous reformation of identities and forms of distinction based around lifestyles, are a defining feature of contemporary consumer society. They give rise to a host of contradictions that manifest themselves in the anxieties and discontents that accompany the late modern condition. The post-war cohorts who participated in the construction of these practices carry their generational habitus with them into later life age. They retain their propensities to be *active consumers* in a society where the construction of identity is as much related to the pursuit of particular commodities as it is to labour market status. Using data from the Family Expenditure Survey, we have tried to show that consumption in later life is uneven. Indeed, consumers are differentiated in terms of their social location, income and wealth and there are apparent differences in terms of cohort and generation. What is clear from the data is that there are consistent patterns of convergence among older cohorts and the rest of the working population. Inequalities both in terms of income and consumption remain, but it is no longer possible to define later life as a period dominated by poverty and exclusion from society. The experience of poverty and exclusion in later life is tied to the lifecourse experiences of individuals who were likely to have experienced accumulated deprivation over earlier parts of the lifecourse. Overall, the direction of engagement with consumer society by older people is towards greater involvement. To date, this is an area of social life that has been largely ignored by social gerontologists and has only recently been taken up by those engaged in marketing and advertising – a reflection, perhaps, of the continued strength of ageist thinking.

It is sometimes, mistakenly, assumed that pointing out the increasing engagement of older groups with consumer society indicates approval of the market solutions to social problems or a disregard for the excesses of consumer capitalism. Our aim in this book was to chart trends in later life rather than to make moral judgements about those trends. As advocates of free market capitalism such as Francis Fukuyama (1992) point out, it is the very richness of the choices that are made available by consumer capitalism that legitimates the economic system and allows for the polymorphous area of *choice* to be equated with principles of freedom and democracy. The pursuit of choice as an end in itself is a fundamental part of the project of constructing the consumer citizen and is seen as an innately positive development (Giddens, 2007, p 8). But as many recognise, such choices are loaded and an excess of choice is not necessarily beneficial to well-being (Schwartz et al, 2002; Offer, 2006). As Ginsborg (2005) points out, these contradictions are based on a dominant neoliberal ideology that, in tandem with the cumulative effects of present social arrangements, is profoundly negative both in terms of its impact on the global environment and on levels of poverty in the developing world. But Ginsborg goes further to point out that a fundamentalist po-faced approach to material consumption ignores the extent to which every new age constructs new desires and needs. There may be new ways of resisting the excesses of mass consumption based around the tactics of daily life (de Certeau, 1988) or on the construction of 'a new erotics of consumption' (Soper and Trentmann, 2007). Indeed, older groups, just as they participated in the new social movements and protest groups of the late 1960s, may have a key role to play in such acts of resistance. But all this would be the subject of another book. In this volume, our aim has been to underline the view that present-day older consumers are constructed across the lifecourse and have engaged with later life through the lens of their generational experiences. This has important implications for the development of the worlds of welfare in the 21st century.

Worlds of welfare and the consumer citizen

As we have seen, health and social care policies for older people have been profoundly affected by the shift in emphasis towards choice and competition in welfare provision. This is a consequence of the general neoliberal shift in social policy that draws on a sense of crisis in welfare and a questioning of the role of the state (Taylor-Gooby, 1998). Previous notions of solidarity and universality are being undermined by an increasing emphasis on individual agency and responsibility. One of the areas where a sense of crisis is most acute is that of pension provision. Many of those entering retirement in the UK receive a significant portion of their income from non-state sources – a mixture of occupational/personal pension schemes and investment income (DWP, 2003). The significance of pension fund capitalism for the global economy has been noted by Blackburn (1999, 2002), as it puts a premium on share price and shareholder value above all else. Although occupational pension schemes have traditionally been tied to the salary level of the pension holder, they have always relied on investing their contributions in order to meet current and future demand. All non-state pension schemes are obliged to operate through financial markets. Although such 'third-pillar' schemes have been strongly supported by international financial institutions such as the World Bank, their success in assuring prosperity throughout post-working life relies heavily on the success of the global economy. The long-term future of taxation-based and investment-based retirement incomes are far from assured. Each faces a number of dilemmas. First is the sustainability of an inter-generational compact for state retirement pensions in the UK, whereby under pay-as-you-go arrangements today's pensioners rely on the success of the national economy in order to secure their share of the productivity of labour. Increasing prosperity for most of the last half century has meant that both workers and pensioners in affluent countries have not only seen their living standards rise, but have avoided dilemmas of generational inequity discussed in collections such as Johnson and colleagues' (1989) *Workers versus pensioners*. In part, this might be because of the low levels of state retirement pension in the UK, but it may also be due to the absence of such a serious economic crisis such as that occasioned by the Wall Street crash of 1929 undermining the compact that still remains popular (Walker and Maltby, 1997). To date, even the declining fortunes of those working in traditional industries, who have experienced high levels of unemployment and seen many jobs disappear, have not led to any desire to claw back resources from the retired population. At the time of writing, however, there are worries of economic recession that may have profound consequences for inter-generational reciprocity. Moving away from the state retirement pension, the sustainability of rising retirement income derived from capital owned by pension funds depends on more than the post-war inter-generational compact, however stable that may be. This brings us to the second crucial factor, namely the future of world markets. Pension funds represent an ever-larger share of total world assets, and are fast becoming the dominant form of capital investment throughout the world (Blackburn, 1999, p 5). For some, this was one of the principal reasons for the rise in share value during the 1990s, as more and more funds chased short-term investment opportunities (Minns, 2001). For a long period of time, pension funds have drawn in more money than they have had to pay out as growing numbers of workers have contributed record amounts in line with their rising affluence. As the numbers of workers retiring begin to exceed the size of the numbers joining the workforce, the easy expansion of the numbers covered by pension funds themselves comes under threat. Already there have been considerable changes to occupational pensions, with benefits being calculated in terms of the size of the sums contributed rather than in terms of highest salary levels as had been traditionally the case (Minns, 2006). Although this will not affect those already in retirement, it does suggest that among future retirees the increasing individualisation and diversification of post-working life that we have already described in this book will become more pronounced.

There are many accounts of why there has been a shift away from universalistic forms of welfare to more individualistic ones. Apart from an obvious change in political approach that accompanied the electoral victories of both Margaret Thatcher in the UK and Ronald Reagan in the US, there is also the fact that basic ideas of citizenship have been transformed by consumerism so that a failure to be an agentic consumer in your own right is to be seen as a failure in society

(Bauman, 1998). To have choices made for you is to yield social status. This focus on choice and agency has been at the root of the success of New Labour and of its reconceptualisation of connection between state and citizen (Giddens, 2007). Enabling the citizen to achieve socially desirable outcomes is now seen as the state's task and with the provision of input capable of producing these aims comes responsibilities and duties.

In these circumstances, there is increasing pressure on welfare state systems to transform themselves along market lines, either through the introduction of privatisation or through quasi-markets. Forms of welfare that emphasise solidarity and decommodification are considered anachronistic and therefore legitimate targets for reform. The UK state retirement pension is one case in point. Its universalism and flat-rate benefits are seen as only fit to be part of an anti-poverty policy and not a key entitlement of citizenship. Current government policy on pensions is to mandate individuals and employers to enter the private sector, thereby relieving the state of responsibility of what was once a key part of social policy.

However, neoliberal policies on welfare do not solve the contradictions the welfare state was set up to deal with. As Offe (2007) argues, capitalist welfare states are still caught by a dual compulsion to secure favourable conditions for capitalist reproduction and, by virtue of having democratic forms, to secure legitimacy. The former compulsion requires the pursuit of strategies of recommodification (for example, privatisation of social care) but the latter leaves the door open for decommodification. These contradictory imperatives mean that the welfare state is prone to periodic crisis, with its agents continually caught up in crisis management activities. Furthermore, Offe argues, the neoliberal goal of shrinking the role of the state would lead to problems of delegitimation as increased problems of governability arise. Drawing on the French regulation school, Jessop (2007) suggests that the social institutions, networks and norms that stabilised capitalism under the Fordist mode of accumulation depended on a state committed to the goals of full employment and mass consumption that were consistent with Fordist modes of regulation. Recent transformations in forms of production, technology and communication have led to new conditions of capitalism based around flexible labour markets, segmented markets and more differentiated forms of consumption. Looked at from this perspective, the welfare state faces a new and distinctive mode of economic regulation rather than intervention. Pressures on welfare systems therefore have increasingly been formed around the need to subordinate social policy to the needs of post-Fordist forms based around labour market flexibility and global markets. According to some observers of welfare systems, this means that there is an increasing incompatibility between welfare system design and welfare systems goals. The reality of relative affluence among many of the EU's older population has led many social democrat-inclined thinkers to identify a growing generational imbalance in welfare provision that can only be rectified by shifting provision from the retired to young families

(Esping-Andersen, 2002). It is indeed ironic that the origins of many current problems of many European welfare states lie in their success in creating the conditions for an expanding consumer society. In particular, in reducing poverty in later life, many nations such as France, Germany and Italy have now got to square the demands of a relatively well-off older population with the needs of a discontented younger population. In the UK, the shift to more privatised forms of social security in later life has had the impact of placing responsibility for dealing with the vagaries of both financial and housing markets on government – with the clear expectation that this is now its duty.

Conclusion

Our focus in this book has been on the last 40 years of the 20th century. In particular, we have focused on the growing engagement of older people with consumer society and we have tried to place these patterns within a theoretical framework that draws on two strands of modern thought: the concept of generation as seen from the perspective of generational habitus and generational field and the rise of the individualised consumer citizen in the context of late modernity. What we have highlighted are simple trends and within these trends there are patterns of unevenness, inequality and contradiction. However, we believe that there is sufficient evidence to highlight the need for further research on consumption in later life, covering a host of areas from the construction of lifestyles in retirement, the meanings attributed to certain goods and the capacity of certain consumer goods to enhance capacities to live the good life in old age. For the present, however, it seems clear that we can conclude that older people can no longer be seen as passive observers of consumer culture or a residual category outside of it. For better or worse, they have been and are actively engaged in its production and reproduction.

References

Abrams, M. (1951) *Social surveys and social action*, London: Heinemann.

Abrams, P. (1970) 'Rites de passage: the conflict of generations in industrial society', *Journal of Contemporary History*, vol 5, pp 175-90.

Abrams, P. (1982) *Historical sociology*, New York, NY: Cornell University Press.

ADI (Alzheimer's Disease International) (1999) *The prevalence of dementia: Fact sheet 3*, London: Alzheimer's Disease International.

Äijänseppä, S., Notkola, I.-L., Tijhuis, M., van Staveren, W., Kromhaut, D. and Nissinen, A. (2005) 'Physical functioning in elderly Europeans: 10 year changes in the north and south: the HALE project', *Journal of Epidemiology and Community Health*, vol 59, pp 413-19.

Allen, R. and Bewley, A. (1935) *Family expenditure: A study of its variation*, London: P.S. King & Son.

Al-Windi, A., Elmfeldt, D. and Svardsudd, K. (2000) 'The relationship between age, gender, well-being and symptoms, and the use of pharmaceuticals, herbal medicines and self-care products in a Swedish municipality', *European Journal of Clinical Pharmacology*, vol 56, no 4, pp 311-17.

Andersen, L.B. and Blegvad, M. (2006) 'Does ownership matter for the delivery of professionalized public services? Cost efficiency and effectiveness in private and public dental care for children in Denmark', *Public Administration*, vol 84, no 1, pp 147-64.

Anderson, B. (1988) *Imagined communities*, London: Verso.

Anderson, M. (1985) 'The emergence of the modern life cycle in Britain', *Social History*, vol 10, no 1, pp 69-87.

Andrews, G. (2002) 'Private complementary medicine and older people: service use and user empowerment', *Ageing & Society*, vol 22, no 3, pp 343-68.

Andrews, G. (2003) 'Placing the consumption of private complementary medicine: everyday geographies of older peoples' use', *Health & Place*, vol 9, no 4, pp 337-49.

Andrews, R. and Martin, S. (2007) 'Has devolution improved public services?', *Public Money & Management*, 27, vol 2, pp 149-56.

Appleby, J., Harrison, A. and Devlin, N. (2003) *What is the real cost of more patient choice?*, London: King's Fund.

Arber, S. (1991) 'Class, paid employment and family roles: making sense of structural disadvantage, gender and health status', *Social Science & Medicine*, vol 32, no 4, pp 425-36.

Arber, S. and Attias-Donfut, C. (1999) *The myth of generational conflict*, London: Routledge.

Arber, S. and Ginn, J. (1993) 'Gender and inequalities in health in later life', *Social Science & Medicine*, vol 36, no 1, pp 33-46.

Arber, S. and Lahelma, E. (1993) 'Inequalities in women's and men's ill-health – Britain and Finland compared', *Social Science & Medicine*, vol 37, no 8, pp 1055-68.

Atkinson, A. (1999) 'The distribution of income in the UK and OECD countries in the twentieth century', *Oxford Review of Economic Policy*, vol 15, no 4, pp 56-75.

Atkinson, A.B. (2000) 'Distribution of income and wealth', in A.H. Halsey and J. Webb (eds) *Twentieth-century British social trends*, Basingstoke: Macmillan.

Audit Commission (1985) *Managing social services for the elderly more effectively*, London: HMSO.

Audit Commission (1986) *Making a reality of community care*, London: HMSO.

Baldwin, S. and Corden, A. (1987) 'Public money and private care: paradoxes and problems', in S. di Gregorio (ed) *Social gerontology: New directions*, Beckenham: Croom Helm, pp 90-103.

Ball, C. (2002) 'Reflections on the third age', *Quality in Ageing*, vol 3, no 2, pp 3-5.

Ballantyne, P., Clark, P., Marshman, J., Victor, C. and Fisher, J. (2005) 'Use of prescribed and non-prescribed medicines by the elderly: implications for who chooses, who pays and who monitors the risk of medicines', *International Journal of Pharmacy Practice*, vol 13, no 2, pp 133-40.

Banks, J. and Leicester, A. (2006) 'Expenditure and consumption', in J. Banks, E. Breeze, C. Lessof and J. Nazroo (eds) *Retirement, health and relationships of the older population in England: The 2004 English Longitudinal Study of Ageing, Wave 2*, London: Institute of Fiscal Studies, pp 243-63.

Barat, I., Andreasen, F. and Damsgaard, E. (2000) 'The consumption of drugs by 75-year-old individuals living in their own homes', *European Journal of Clinical Pharmacology*, vol 56, nos 6-7, pp 501-9.

Bardasi, E., Jenkins, S.P. and Rigg, J.A. (2002) 'Retirement and the income of older people: a British perspective', *Ageing & Society*, vol 22, no 3, pp 131-59.

Barker, G. and Hancock, R. (2000) 'The income dimension', in D. Hirsch (ed) *Life after fifty: Issues for policy and research*, York: York Publishing Services.

Barnes, M., Blom, A., Cox, K. and Lessof, C. (2006) *The social exclusion of older people: Evidence from the first wave of the English Longitudinal Study of Ageing (ELSA), Final Report*, London: The Stationery Office.

Bauman, Z. (1995) *Life in fragments*, Cambridge: Polity.

Bauman, Z. (1998) *Work, consumerism and the new poor*, Buckingham: Open University Press.

Bauman, Z. (2000) *Liquid modernity*, Cambridge: Polity.

Bauman, Z. (2007) *Consuming life*, Cambridge: Polity.

BBC News (2008) 'Older people's champion for Wales', 7 January (http://news.bbc.co.uk, downloaded 6 June 2008).

Bebbington, A. and Tong, M.-S. (1986) 'Trends and changes in old people's homes: provision over twenty years', in K. Judge and I. Sinclair (eds) *Residential care for elderly people*, London: HMSO.

Beck, U. (1991) *Risk society*, London: Sage Publications.

Beck, U. (2000) *The brave new world of work*, Cambridge: Polity.

Beck, U., Bonss, W. and Lau, C. (2003) 'The theory of reflexive modernization: problematic, hypotheses and research programme', *Theory, Culture and Society*, vol 20, no 2, pp 1-33.

Beck, U., Giddens, A. and Lash, S. (1994) *Reflexive modernisation: Politics, tradition and aesthetics in the modern social order*, Cambridge: Polity.

Becker, H. (1991) 'A pattern of generations and its consequences', in H.A. Becker (ed) *Dynamics of cohort and generations research*, Amsterdam: Thesis Publishers.

Beckett, M. (2000) 'Converging health inequalities in later life – an artefact of mortality selection?', *Journal of Health and Social Behaviour*, vol 41, no 1, pp 106-9.

Bédarida, F. (1979) *A social history of England, 1851-1975*, London: Methuen.

Bell, K.M. (1965) 'The development of community care', *Public Administration*, vol 43, 4, pp 419-35.

Bengston, V. and Putney, N. (2006) 'Future "conflicts" across generations and cohorts?', in J. Vincent, C. Phillipson and M. Downs (eds) *The futures of old age*, London: Sage Publications.

Bennett, G. (1999) 'Institutional abuse of older people', *International Journal of Therapy and Rehabilitation*, vol 6, no 9, pp 420-2.

Benson, J. (1994) *The rise of consumer society in Britain, 1880-1980*, London: Longman.

Blackburn, R. (1999) 'The new collectivism: pension reform, grey capitalism and complex socialism', *New Left Review*, vol 233, January-February, pp 3-65.

Blackburn, R. (2002) *Banking on death or investing in life: The history and future of pensions*, London: Verso.

Blane, D., Higgs, P., Hyde, M. and Wiggins, R. (2004) 'Life course influences on quality of life in early old age', *Social Science & Medicine*, vol 58, no 11, pp 2171-9.

Blöndal, S. and Scarpetta, S. (1999) *The retirement decision in OECD countries*, OECD Economics Department Working Paper No 202, Paris: Organisation for Economic Co-operation and Development.

Blow, L., Leicester, A. and Oldfield, Z. (2004) *Consumption trends in the UK, 1975-99*, London: Institute of Fiscal Studies.

Blundell, R. and Preston, I. (1998) 'Consumption inequality and income uncertainty,' *The Quarterly Journal of Economics*, vol 113, no 2, pp 603-40.

Bocock, R. (1993) *Consumption*, London: Routledge.

Booth, T., Barritt, A., Berry, S., Martin, D. and Melotte, C. (1983) 'Dependency in residential homes for the elderly', *Social Policy and Administration*, vol 17, no 1, pp 46-63.

Bourdieu, P. (1977) *Outline of a theory of practice*, Cambridge: Cambridge University Press.

Bourdieu, P. and Wacquant, L. (1996) *An invitation to reflexive sociology*, Cambridge: Polity.

Breeze, E., Sloggett, A. and Fletcher, A.E. (1999) 'Socioeconomic status and transition in old age in relation to limiting long-term illness measured at the 1991 Census. Results of the Longitudinal Study', *European Journal of Public Health*, vol 9, no 4, pp 265-70.

Breeze, E., Fletcher, A.E., Leon, D.A., Marmot, M.G., Clarke, R.J. and Shipley, M.J. (2001) 'Do socioeconomic disadvantages persist into old age? Self-reported morbidity in a 29-year follow-up of the Whitehall Study', *American Journal of Public Health*, vol 91, no 2, pp 277-83.

Brooker, C. (1970) The neophiliacs: Revolution in English life in the fifties and sixties, London: Fontana.

Brown, R.L. and Prus, S.G. (2006) 'Income inequality over the later life course: a comparative analysis of seven OECD countries', *Annals of Actuarial Science*, vol 1, no 2, pp 307-17.

Bury, M. (1995) 'Ageing, gender and sociological theory', in S. Arber and J. Ginn (eds) *Connecting ageing and gender: A sociological approach*, Buckingham: Open University Press.

Calasanti, T. (2003) 'Work and retirement in the 21st century: integrating issues of diversity and globalization', *Ageing International*, vol 28, no 3, pp 3-20.

Calnan, M. and Gabe, J. (2001) 'From consumerism to partnership? Britain's National Health Service at the turn of the century', *International Journal of Health Services*, vol 31, no 1, pp 119-31.

Capuzzo, P. (2001) 'Youth culture and consumption in contemporary Europe', *Contemporary European History*, vol 10, no 1, pp 155-70.

Carnegie Inquiry (1993) *Life, work and livelihood in the third age*, Dunfermline: Carnegie UK Trust.

Carnegie Inquiry (2000) *A decade of progress and change: A report on ten years' activity and action on the third age*, Dunfermline: Carnegie UK Trust.

Carvel, J. (2007) 'Councils turn backs on care for older people', *The Guardian*, 22 November, p 4.

Casey, B. and Yamada, A. (2002) *Getting older, getting poorer? A study of the earnings, pensions, assets and living arrangements of older people in nine countries*, Labour Market and Social Policy Occasional Papers No 60, Paris: Organisation for Economic Co-operation and Development.

Casey, B. and Yamada, A. (2003) 'The public–private mix of retirement income in nine OECD countries: some evidence from micro-data and an exploration of its implications', in M. Rein and W. Schmaehl (eds) *Rethinking the welfare state: The political economy of pension reform*, Cheltenham: Edward Elgar.

Castells, M. (1996) *The rise of the network society*, Oxford: Blackwell.

Charlesworth, A., Wilkin, D. and Durie, A. (1984) *Carers and services: A comparison of men and women caring for dependent elderly people*, Manchester: Equal Opportunities Commission.

Chen, Y., Dewey, M., Avery, A. and the Analysis Group of the MRCCFA Study (2001) 'Self-reported medication use for older people in England and Wales', *Journal of Clinical Pharmacy Therapeutics*, vol 26, no 2, pp 129-40.

Clarke, J., Smith, N. and Vidler, E. (2005) 'Consumerism and the reform of public services, inequalities and instabilities', in M. Powell, L. Bauld and K. Clarke (eds) *Social Policy Review*, vol 17, pp 167-82.

Conway, S. and Hockey, J. (1998) 'Resisting the "mask" of old age?: the social meaning of lay health beliefs in later life', *Ageing & Society*, vol 18, no 4, pp 469-94.

Cook, F. and Settersten, R. (1995) 'Expenditure patterns by age and income among mature adults: does age matter?', *The Gerontologist*, vol 35, no 1, pp 10-23.

Corsten, M. (1999) 'The time of generations', *Time & Society*, vol 8, no 2, pp 249-72.

Cutler, N. (1977) 'Political socialization research as generational analysis: the cohort approach versus the lineage approach', in S.A. Renshon (ed) *Handbook of political socialization*, New York, NY: Free Press.

Dahl, S.-A., Nilsen, Ø.A. and Vage, K. (2003) 'Gender differences in early retirement behaviour', *European Sociological Review*, vol 19, no 2, pp 179-98.

Danesi, M. (2003) *Forever young: The 'teenaging' of modern culture*, Toronto: University of Toronto Press.

Dannefer, D. (2003) 'Cumulative advantage/disadvantage and the life course: cross-fertilizing age and social science theory', *Journals of Gerontology Series B: Psychological Sciences and Social Sciences*, vol 58, S327-S338.

Darton, R. and Wright, K. (1992) 'Residential and nursing homes for elderly people: one sector or two?', in F. Laczko and C.R. Victor (eds) *Social policy and elderly people*, Aldershot: Avebury, pp 216-44.

Davies, B. (1987) 'New managerialist argument and the supply and financing of care', in S. di Gregario (ed) *Social gerontology: New directions*, Beckenham: Croom Helm, pp 75-89.

de Certeau, M. (1988) *The practice of everyday life*, Berkley, CA: University of California Press.

Deeming, C. and Keen, J. (2002) 'Paying for old age: can people on lower incomes afford domiciliary care costs?', *Social Policy and Administration*, vol 36, no 5, pp 465-81.

Deeming, C. and Keen, J. (2003) 'A fair deal for care in older age? Public attitudes towards the funding of long-term care', *Policy and Politics*, vol 31, no 4, p 431.

del Bono, E., Sala, E., Hancock, R., Gunnell, C. and Parisi, L. (2007) *Gender, older people and social exclusion: Gendered review and secondary analyses of the data*, ISER Working Paper 2007-13, Colchester: University of Essex.

Denning, M. (2004) *Culture in the age of the three worlds*, London: Verso.

DH (Department of Health) (1989) *Caring for people: Community care in the next decade and beyond*, London: HMSO.

DH (1990) *NHS Community Care Act*, London: HMSO.

DH (1995) *Carers (Recognition and Services) Act*, London: HMSO.

DH (1996) *Community Care (Direct Payments) Act*, London: The Stationery Office.

DH (1997) *The new NHS: Modern, dependable*, London: The Stationery Office.

DH (1999) *Saving lives: Our healthier nation*, London: The Stationery Office.

DH (2000a) *The NHS plan*, London: The Stationery Office.

DH (2000b) *Community Care (Direct Payments) Act 1996: Policy and practice guidance*, London: The Stationery Office.

DH (2003) *The National Service Framework for Older People*, London: The Stationery Office.

DH (2005) *Independence, well-being and choice, our vision for the future of social care in England*, London: The Stationery Office.

DH (2006) *Our health, our care, our say: A new direction for community services*, London: The Stationery Office.

DH (2007) *Putting people first: A shared vision and commitment to the transformation of adult social care*, London: The Stationery Office. (www.dh.gov.uk/en/Publicationsandstatistics/Publications/PublicationsPolicyAndGuidance/DH_081118, accessed 10 December).

Disney, R.R. and Whitehouse, E. (2001) *Cross-country comparisons of pensioners' incomes*, Research Report No 142, London: Department of Social Security.

Dixon, M. and Margo, J. (2006) *Population politics*, London: Institute for Public Policy Research.

Donkin, A., Goldblatt, P. and Lynch, P. (2002) 'Inequalities in life expectancy by social class, 1972-1999', *Health Statistics Quarterly*, vol 15, Autumn, pp 5-15.

Dorling, D., Rigby, J., Wheeler, B., Ballas, D., Thomas, B., Fahmy, E., Gordon, D. and Lupton, R. (2007) *Poverty and wealth across Britain, 1968 to 2005*, York: Joseph Rowntree Foundation.

Dunn, E. and Gibbins, C. (eds) (2006) *Family spending 2006*, Basingstoke: Macmillan.

Dupre, M.E. (2007) 'Educational differences in age-related patterns of diseases: reconsidering the cumulative disadvantage and age-as-leveller hypothesis', *Journal of Health and Social Behaviour*, vol 48, no 1, pp 1-15.

DWP (Department for Work and Pensions) (2003) *Pensioner Income Series 2001/02*, London: The Stationery Office.

DWP (2006) *Pensioners' Income Series 2005/06*, London: DWP.

DWP (2007) *Pensioners' Income Series 2005/06 (Revised)*, London: Office for National Statistics.

Dychtwald, K. (1999) *Age power: How the 21st century will be ruled by the new old*, New York, NY: Jeremy P. Tarcher/Putnam.

Edmunds, J. and Turner, B.S. (2002) *Generations, Culture and Society*, Buckingham: Open University Press.

Ekert-Jaffé, O. (1989) 'Vieillissement et consummation: quelques résultats tirés des enquêtes françaises sur les budgets des ménages', *Population*, vol 44, no 3, pp 561-579.

Ernest, E. and White, A. (2000) 'The BBC survey of complementary medicine use in the UK', *Complementary Therapies in Medicine*, vol 8, 1, pp 32-6.

Esping-Andersen, G. (2000) 'The sustainability of welfare states into the twenty-first century', *International Journal of Health Services*, vol 30, no 1, pp 1-12.

Esping-Andersen, G. (2002) *Why we need a new welfare state*, Oxford: Oxford University Press.

Estes, C.L. (1979) *The aging enterprise*, San Francisco, CA: Jossey-Bass.

Estes, C.L. (2001) *Social policy and aging: A critical perspective*, London: Sage Publications.

European Commission (2000) *Social policy agenda, COM (2000)*, Brussels: European Commission.

Evandrou, M. (2005) *Health and well-being amongst older people in Britain at the start of the 21st century*, SAGE Research Group Discussion Paper 22, London: London School of Economics.

Evandrou, M. and Falkingham, J. (2000) 'Looking back to look forwards: lessons from four birth cohorts for ageing in the 21st century', *Population Trends*, vol 99, Spring, pp 21-30.

Evandrou, M. and Falkingham, J. (2002) 'Smoking behaviour and socioeconomic status: a cohort analysis, 1974 to 1998', *Health Statistics Quarterly*, vol 14, Summer, pp 30-8.

Even, W.E. and Macpherson, D.A. (1990) 'The gender gap in pensions and wages', *Review of Economics and Statistics*, vol 72, no 2, pp 259-65.

Fairchilds, C. (1993) 'Consumption in early modern Europe: a review article', *Comparative Studies in Society and History*, vol 35, no 4, pp 850-8.

Featherstone, M. and Hepworth, M. (1998) 'Ageing, the lifecourse and the sociology of embodiment', in G. Scambler and P. Higgs (eds) *Modernity, medicine and health*, London: Routledge.

Ferlie, E., Challis, D. and Davies, B. (1985) 'Innovation in the care of the elderly: the role of joint finance', in A. Butler (ed) *Ageing: Recent advances and creative responses*, Croom Helm: Beckenham, pp 137-59.

Förster, M. (2000) *Trends and driving factors in income distribution and poverty in the OECD area*, Labour Market and Social Policy Occasional Papers No 42, Paris: Organisation for Economic Co-operation and Development.

Foucault, M. (1988) 'Technologies of the self', in L.H. Martin, H. Gutman and P.H. Hutton (eds) *Technologies of the self: A seminar with Michel Foucault*, London: Tavistock.

Fox, A.J. and Goldblatt, P. (1982) *Longitudinal study: Socio-demographic mortality differentials*, London: HMSO.

Freedman, M. (1999) *Prime time: How baby boomers will revolutionize retirement and transform America*, New York, NY: Public Affairs.

Freeman, J. (2004) *The making of the modern kitchen*, Oxford: Berg.

Fukuyama, F. (1992) *The end of history and the last man*, Harmondsworth: Penguin Books.

Gastwirth, J.L. (1972) 'The estimation of the Lorenz curve and the Gini coefficient', *The Review of Economics and Statistics*, vol 54, no 3, pp 306-16.

Gazeley, I. (2003) *Poverty in Britain, 1900-1965*, London: Palgrave.

Gee, E. and Gutman, G. (2000) 'Population and politics: voodoo demography, population aging and social policy', in E. Gee, and G. Gutman (eds) *The overselling of population aging: Apocalyptic demography, intergenerational challenges, and social policy*, Oxford: Oxford University Press.

Gerhard, D. (1973) 'Periodization in history', in P.P. Weiner (ed) *Dictionary of the history of ideas, studies of selected pivotal ideas*, vol 2, pp 456-64 New York: Charles Scribner's Sons.

Giddens, A. (1991) *Modernity and self-identity, self and society in the late modern age*, Cambridge: Polity.

Giddens, A. (1994) *Beyond Left and Right*, Cambridge: Polity.

Giddens A. (1998) *The third way*, Cambridge: Polity.

Giddens, A. (2007) *Over to you, Mr Brown*, Cambridge: Polity.

Gilbert, N. (2002) *The transformation of the welfare state, the silent surrender of public responsibility*, Oxford: Oxford University Press.

Gilleard, C. (1996) 'Consumption and identity in later life: toward a cultural gerontology', *Ageing & Society*, 16, no 4, pp 489-98.

Gilleard, C. and Higgs, P. (1998) 'Older people as users and consumers of health care: a third age rhetoric for a fourth age reality', *Ageing & Society*, vol 18, no 2, pp 233-48.

Gilleard, C. and Higgs, P. (2000) *Cultures of ageing: Self, citizen and the body*, Harlow: Prentice Hall.

Gilleard, C. and Higgs, P. (2005) *Contexts of ageing: Class, cohort and community*, Cambridge: Polity.

Ginn, J. (2001) *From security to risk: Pension privatisation and gender inequality*, London: Catalyst.

Ginn, J., Street, D. and Arber, S. (2002) (eds) *Women, work and pensions*, Milton Keynes: Open University Press.

Ginsborg, P. (2005) *The politics of everyday life. Making choices, changing lives*, New Haven, CT: Yale University Press.

Goodman, A. and Oldfield, Z. (2004) *Permanent differences? Income and expenditure inequality in the 1990s and 2000s*, Institute of Fiscal Studies Report 66, London: Institute of Fiscal Studies.

Gould, N. and Gould, E. (2001) 'Health as a consumption object: research notes and preliminary investigation', *International Journal of Consumer Studies*, vol 25, no 2, pp 90-101.

Greener, I. (2008) 'Choice and voice: a review', *Social Policy and Society*, vol 7, no 2, pp 255-65.

Greer, G. (1991) *The Change*, Harmondsworth: Penguin Books.

Greer, S.L. (2004) 'The politics of health policy divergence', Paper presented at IPPR seminar, Edinburgh, 16 September.

Griffiths, R. (1988) *Community care: Agenda for action. A report to the Secretary of State for Social Services by Sir Roy Griffiths*, London: The Stationery Office.

Grint, K. (1998) *The sociology of work* (2nd edn), Cambridge: Polity.

Grundy, E. and Glaser, K. (2000) 'Socio-demographic differences in the onset and progression of disability in early old age: a longitudinal study', *Age and Ageing*, vol 29, no 2, pp 149-57.

Grundy, E. and Sloggett, A. (2003) 'Health inequalities in the older population: the role of personal capital, social resources and socio-economic circumstances', *Social Science & Medicine*, vol 56, no 5, pp 935-47.

Gunn, S. and Bell, R. (2002) *Middle classes: Their rise and sprawl*, London: Cassell & Co.

Gunter, B. (1998) *Understanding the older consumer: The grey market*, London: Routledge.

Hakim, C. (2000) *Work–lifestyle choices in the 21st century: Preference theory*, Oxford: Oxford University Press.

Halsey, A.H. and Webb, J. (2000) *Twentieth-century British social trends*, Basingstoke: Macmillan.

Hardy, M.A. and Waite, L. (1997) 'Doing time: reconciling biography with history in the study of social change', in M.A. Hardy (ed) *Studying aging and social change*, London: Sage Publications.

Harvey, D. (1990) *The condition of postmodernity: An inquiry into the origins of cultural change*, Oxford: Blackwell.

Hazlett, J.D. (1998) *My generation: Collective autobiography and identity politics*, Madison, WI: University of Wisconsin Press.

Hebdidge, D. (1979) *Subculture: The meaning of style*, London: Methuen.

Held, D., McGrew, A.G., Goldblatt, D. and Perraton, J. (1999) *Global transformations: Politics, economics, and culture*, Cambridge: Polity.

Higgs, P. (1993) *The NHS and ideological conflict*, Aldershot: Avebury.

Higgs, P. (1995) 'Citizenship and old age: the end of the road?', *Ageing & Society*, vol 15, no 5, pp 535-50.

Hills, J. (2004) *Inequality and the state*, Oxford: Oxford University Press.

Hills, J. and Stewart, K. (2005) *A more equal society? New Labour, poverty, inequality and exclusion*, Bristol: The Policy Press.

Hine, T. (2000) *The rise and fall of the American teenager*, New York, NY: HarperCollins.

Holmans, A. (2000) 'Housing', in A.H. Halsey and J. Webb (eds) *Twentieth-century British social trends*, Basingstoke: Macmillan.

Hood, C. (1991) 'A public management for all seasons?', *Public Administration*, vol 69, no 1, pp 3-19.

Hood, C. (1995) 'The "new public management" in the 1980s: variations on a theme', *Accounting, Organizations and Society*, vol 20, nos 2-3, pp 93-109.

Hungerford, T.L. (2003) 'Is there an American way of aging? Income dynamics of the elderly in the United States and Germany', *Research on Ageing*, vol 25, no 5, pp 435-55.

Hurd, M. (1989) 'The economic status of the elderly', *Science*, vol 244, no 4905, pp 659-64.

Hyde, M. and Jones, I.R. (2007) 'The long shadow of work? Does time since labour market exit affect the association between socio-economic position and health in a post working population?', *Journal of Epidemiology and Community Health*, vol 61, no 6, pp 532-8.

Inglehart, R. (1997) *Modernization and postmodernization: Cultural economic and political change in 43 societies*, Princeton, NJ: Princeton University Press.

Irwin, S. (1999) 'Later life, inequality and sociological theory', *Ageing & Society*, vol 19, no 6, pp 691-715.

Jackson, W.A. (2006) 'Post-Fordism and population aging', *International review of applied economics*, vol 20, no 4, pp 449-67.

Jameson, F. (1991) *Postmodernism, or the cultural logic of late capitalism*, London: Verso.

Jessop, B. (2002) *The future of the capitalist state*, Cambridge: Polity.

Jessop, B. (2007) 'Towards a Schumpterian workfare state? Preliminary remarks on post-Fordist political economy', in R. Vij (ed) *Globalization and welfare: A critical reader*, Basingstoke: Macmillan.

Johnson, D. and Young, J. (2006) 'Costly ageing or costly deaths? Understanding health care expenditure using Australian Medicare payments data', *Australian Economic Papers*, vol 45, no 1, pp 57-74.

Johnson, P., Conrad, C. and Thomson, D. (eds) (1989) *Workers versus pensioners: Intergenerational justice in an ageing world*, Manchester: Manchester University Press.

Jones, I.R. (2003) 'Power, past and present: towards a historical sociology of health and illness', *Social Theory and Health*, vol 1, no 2, pp 130-48.

Kahn, J.R. and Pearlin, L.J. (2006) 'Financial strain over the life course and health among older adults', *Journal of Health and Social Behaviour*, vol 47, no 1, pp 17-31.

Kammen, M. (1999) *American culture, American tastes: Social change and the 20th century*, New York, NY: Basic Books.

Karp, F. (ed) (2007) *Growing older in America: The Health and Retirement Survey*, Washington, DC: National Institute on Aging.

Katznelson, I. (2002) 'Periodization and preferences: reflections on purposive action in comparative-historical social science', in J. Mahoney and D. Rueschemeyer (eds) *Comparative historical analysis in the social sciences*, Cambridge: Cambridge University Press.

Kelner, M. and Wellman, B. (1997) 'Health care and consumer choice: medical and alternative therapies', *Social Science & Medicine*, vol 45, no 2, pp 203-12.

Kertzer, D. (1983) 'Generation as a sociological problem', *Annual Review of Sociology*, vol 9, pp 125-49.

Kohli, M. (1986) 'Social organisation and subjective construction of the lifecourse', in A. Sorensen, F. Weinhart and L. Sherrod (eds) *Human development: Multidisciplinary perspectives*, Hillsdale, NJ: Laurence Erlbaum.

Kotlikoff, L.J. (2003) *Generational policy*, Cambridge, MA: MIT Press.

Kramper, P. (2000) *From economic convergence to convergence in affluence? Income growth, household expenditure and the rise of mass consumption in Britain and West Germany, 1950-1974*, Working Paper 56/00, London: London School of Economics.

Lash, S. and Urry, J. (1987) *The end of organized capitalism*, Cambridge: Polity.

Laslett, P. (1996) *A fresh map of life: The emergence of the third age* (2nd edn), Basingstoke: Macmillan.

Latour, B. (1995) *We have never been modern*, London: Harvester Wheatsheaf.

Latour, B. (2003) 'Is re-modernization occurring – and if so, how to prove it?', *Theory, Culture & Society*, vol 20, no 2, pp 35-48.

Lee, M. (1993) *Consumer culture reborn: The cultural politics of consumption*, London: Routledge.

Le Grand, J. (2003) *Motivation, agency and public policy: Of knights, knaves, pawns and queens*, Oxford: Oxford University Press.

Lewis, J. (2007) 'Gender, agency and the "new social settlement": the importance of developing a holistic approach to care policies', *Current Sociology*, vol 55, no 2, pp 271-86.

Lieberman, E.S. (2001) 'Causal inference in historical institutional analysis: a specification of periodization strategies', *Comparative Political Studies*, vol 34, no 9, pp 1011-35.

Mahoney, J. and Rueschemeyer, D. (eds) (2002) *Comparative historical analysis in the social sciences*, Cambridge: Cambridge University Press.

Mann, K. (2006) 'Three steps to heaven? Tensions in the management of welfare: retirement pensions and active consumers', *Journal of Social Policy*, vol 35, no 1, pp 77-96.

Mannheim, K. (1952) 'The problem of generation', in P. Kecskemeti (ed) *Essays on the sociology of knowledge*, London: Routledge.

Manton, K.G. and Gu, X. (2001) 'Changes in the prevalence of chronic disability in the United States black and nonblack population above age 65 from 1982 to 1999', *Proceedings of the National Academy of Sciences of the United States of America*, vol 98, no 11, pp 6354-59.

Marmot, M.G. and Shipley, M.J. (1996) 'Do socioeconomic differences in mortality persist after retirement? 25 year follow up of civil servants from the first Whitehall study', *British Medical Journal*, 313, 7066, pp 1177-80.

Marmot, M., Banks, J., Blundell, R., Lessof, C. and Nazroo, J. (2003) *Health, wealth and lifestyles of the older population of England: The 2002 English Longitudinal Survey of Ageing*, London: Institute of Fiscal Studies.

Marnoch, G. (2003) 'Scottish devolution: identity and impact and the case of community care for the elderly', *Public Administration*, vol 81, no 2, pp 253-73.

Marwick, A. (1998) *The sixties*, Oxford: Oxford University Press.

Marwick, A. (2003) *British society since 1945* (4th edn), London: Penguin Books.

Mayer, K.U., Maas, I. and Wagner, M. (2001) 'Socioeconomic conditions and social inequalities in old age', in P.B. Baltes and K.U. Mayer (eds) *The Berlin Aging Study. Aging from 70 to 100*, Cambridge: Cambridge University Press.

McClements, L.D. (1977) 'Equivalence scales for children', *Journal of Public Economics*, vol 8, no 2, pp 191-210.

McDonald, R. (2006) 'Creating a patient-led NHS: empowering consumers or shrinking state?', in L. Bauld, K. Clarke and T. Maltby (eds) *Social Policy Review*, vol 18, pp 33-48.

McElnay, J. and Dickson, F. (1994) 'Purchases from community pharmacies of OTC medicines by elderly patients', *The Pharmaceutical Journal*, vol 2, no 15.

Means, R. (1986) 'The development of social services for elderly people: Historical perspectives', in C. Phillipson and A. Walker (eds) *Ageing and social policy: A critical assessment*, Aldershot: Gower.

Meara, E., White, C. and Cutler, D.M. (2004) 'Trends in medical spending by age, 1963-2000', *Health Affairs*, vol 23, no 4, pp 176-83.

Metz, D. and Underwood, M. (2005) *Older richer fitter: Identifying the customer needs of Britain's ageing population*, London: Age Concern Books.

Michelon, L.C. (1954) 'The new leisure class', *American Journal of Sociology*, vol 59, no 4, pp 371-8.

Midwinter, E. (2005) 'How many people are there in the third age?', *Ageing & Society*, vol 25, pp 9-18.

Milewa, T., Valentine, J. and Calnan, M. (1999) 'Community participation and citizenship in British health care planning: narratives of power and involvement in the changing welfare state', *Sociology of Health and Illness*, vol 21, no 4, pp 445-65.

Millard, P. and Higgs, P. (1989) 'Geriatric medicine beyond the hospital', *Age and Ageing*, 18, no 1, pp 1-3.

Minns, R. (2001) *The Cold War in welfare: Stock markets versus pensions*, London: Verso.

Minns, R. (2006) 'The future of stock market pensions', in J. Vincent, C. Phillipson and M. Downs (eds) *The futures of old age*, London: Sage Publications.

Mohan, H. (2003) 'Voluntarism, municipalism and welfare: the geography of hospital utilization in England in 1938', *Transactions of the Institute of British Geographers*, vol 28, no 1, pp 56-74.

Murdock, G. and McCron, R. (1976) 'Consciousness of class and consciousness of generation', in S. Hall, J. Clarke, T. Jefferson and B. Roberts (eds) *Resistance through rituals*, London: Hutchinson.

NAO (National Audit Office) (2000) *Hip replacement: Getting it right first time*, London: The Stationery Office.

Needham, C.E. (2006) 'Customer care and the public service ethos', *Public Administration*, vol 84, no 4, pp 845-60.

Neugarten, B.L. (1974) 'Age groups in American society and the rise of the young-old', *Annals of the American Academy of Political and Social Science*, vol 9, pp 187-98.

Nield, Lt. Col. J.C. (1898) *Report on old age pensions, charitable relief and state insurance*, Sydney: Government Printers.

Nisbet, R. (1972) *Social change*, Oxford: Basil Blackwell.

Nixon, S. (1996) *Hard looks: Masculinities, spectatorship and contemporary consumption*, London: UCL Press.

Offe, C. (2007) 'Some contradictions of the modern welfare state', in R.Vij (ed) *Globalizaiton and welfare: A critical reader*, Basingstoke: Macmillan.

Offer, A. (2006) *The challenge of affluence: Self-control and well-being in the United States and Britain since 1950*, Oxford: Oxford University Press.

Oldenziel, R., de la Bruhèze, A.A.A. and de Wit, O. (2005) 'Europe's mediation junction: technology and consumer society in the 20th century', *History and Technology*, vol 21, no 1, pp 107-39.

ONS (Office for National Statistics) (2002a) 'The distribution of real household disposable income', *Social Trends 34*, London: The Stationery Office (www. statistics.gov.uk/STATBASE/ssdataset.asp?vlnk=7438&More=Y, accessed 27 November 2007).

ONS (2002b) *Family spending: A report on the 2000-2001 Family Expenditure Survey*, London: The Stationery Office.

ONS (2002c) *Living in Britain: Results from the 2001 General Household Survey*, London: The Stationery Office.

ONS (2004) *Sport and Leisure, results from the sport and leisure module of the 2002 General Household Survey*, London: The Stationery Office.

ONS (2006) *Family spending: A report on the 2005-2006 Family Expenditure Survey*, London: The Stationery Office.

ONS (2007a) *Family spending, 2006 edition*, London: The Stationery Office.

ONS (2007b) *Variations persist in life expectancy by social class 2002-2005 data released*, London: ONS (www.statistics.gov.uk/pdfdir/le1007.pdf).

ONS/DH (2002) *Community care statistics 2001: Home care services for adults, England*, London: The Stationery Office.

ONS/DH (2004) *Community care statistics 2003: Home care services for adults, England*, London: The Stationery Office.

ONS/DWP (2005) *Focus on Older People*, London: The Stationery Office.

ONS/NHS (2006) *Community care statistics 2005: Home care services for adults, England*, London: NHS Health and Social Care Information Centre, Department of Health.

ONS/NHS (2007) *Community care statistics 2006: Home care services for adults, England*, London: NHS Health and Social Care Information Centre, Department of Health.

Outhwaite, W. (2006) *The future of society*, Oxford: Blackwell Publishing.

Palmore, E. (1978) 'When can age period and cohort be separated?', *Social Forces*, vol 51, no 1, pp 282-95.

Parker, G. (1990) *With due care and attention: A review of the literature on informal care*, London: Family Policy Studies Centre.

Parker, G. and Clarke, H. (1997) *Attitudes and behaviour towards financial planning for care in old age*, Nuffield Community Care Studies Unit, Leicester: University of Leicester.

Parker, M.G., Thorslund, M. and Lundberg, O. (1994) 'Physical function and social class among Swedish oldest-old', *Journals of Gerontology*, vol 49, no 4, S196-S201.

Pensions Commission (2004) *Pensions: Challenges and choices – the first report of the Pensions Commission*, London: The Stationery Office.

Poole, C., Jones, D. and Veitch, B. (1999) 'Relationships between prescription and non-prescription drug use in the elderly population', *Archives of Gerontology and Geriatrics*, vol 28, no 3, pp 259-71.

Potter, J. (1988) 'Consumerism and the public sector: how well does the coat fit?', *Public Administration*, vol 66, no 2, pp 149-64.

Powell, M. and Hewitt, M. (2002) *Welfare state and welfare change*, Milton Keynes: Open University Press.

Propper, C. (2000) 'The demand for private healthcare in the UK', *Journal of Health Economics*, vol 19, 6, pp 855-76.

Prus, S.G. (2007) 'Age, SES, and health: a population level analysis of health inequalities over the lifecourse', *Sociology of Health and Illness*, vol 29, no 2, pp 175-296.

Rahkonen, O. and Takala, P. (1998) 'Social class differences in health and functional disability among older men and women', *International Journal of Health Services*, vol 28, no 3, pp 511-24.

Ransome, P. (2005) *Work, consumption and culture: Affluence and social change in the twentieth century*, London: Sage Publications.

Roberts, Y. (2004) 'Fifty is the new 30...so drop the Zimmer frame jokes', *Observer*, 23 May, p21.

Royal Commission on Long Term Care (1999) *With respect to old age: Long term care – rights and responsibilities*, London: The Stationery Office.

Ryder, N.B. (1997) 'The cohort as a concept in the study of social change', reproduced in M.A. Hardy (ed) *Studying aging and social change*, London: Sage Publications.

Sandbrook, D. (2005) *Never had it so good: A history of Britain from Suez to the Beatles*, London: Abacus.

Sassatelli, R. (2007) *Consumer culture: History, theory and politics*, London: Sage Publications.

Savage, M. (2007) 'Changing social class identities in post-war Britain: perspectives from mass observation', *Sociological Research Online*, vol 12, issue 3 (www.socresonline.org.uk/12/3/6.html).

Scase, R. and Scales, J. (2000) *Fit and fifty*, Swindon: Economic and Social Research Council.

Schuman, H. and Scott, J. (1989) 'Generations and collective memories', *American Sociological Review*, vol 54, pp 359-81.

Schwartz, B., Ward, A., Monterosso, J., Lyubomirsky, S., White, K. and Lehman, D.R. (2002) 'Maximising versus satisficing: happiness is a matter of choice', *Journal of Personality and Social Psychology*, vol 83, no 5, pp 1178-1197.

Scourfield, J., Holland, S. and Young, C. (2008) Social work in Wales since democratic devolution', *Australian Social Work*, vol 61, no 11, pp 42-56.

Seccombe, W. (1993) *Weathering the storm: Working-class families from the Industrial Revolution to the fertility decline*, London: Verso.

Secretary of State for Health (1992) *National Assistance Act 1948 (Choice of Accommodation) Direction 1992*, London: HMSO.

Self, A. and Zealey, L. (eds) (2007) *Social Trends 37*, London: Office for National Statistics (www.statistics.gov.uk/downloads/theme_social/Social_Trends37/Social_Trends_37.pdf, accessed 31 October 2007).

Sen, A.K. (1985) *Commodities and capabilities*, Oxford: Oxford University Press.

Sennett, R. (2006) *The culture of the new capitalism*, New Haven, CT: Yale University Press.

Seshamani, M. and Gray, A. (2004) 'Time to death and health care expenditure', *Age and Ageing*, vol 33, no 6, pp 556-61.

Sheehy, G. (1996) *New passages*, London: HarperCollins.

Sinclair, I. (1988) 'Elderly', in I. Sinclair (ed) *Residential care: The research reviewed*, London: HMSO, pp 241-92.

Smith, C.W. (1992) 'The geography of private residential care', in K. Morgan (ed) *Gerontology: Responding to an ageing society*, London: Jessica Kingsley, pp 99-117.

Smith, D. (1991) *The rise of historical sociology*, Philadelphia, PA: Temple University Press.

Smith, J.S. (1998) 'The strange history of the decade: modernity, nostalgia, and the perils of periodization', *Journal of Social History*, Winter, pp 263-87.

Smith, J.W. and Clurman, A. (1997) *Rocking the ages: The Yankelovich Report on generational marketing*, New York, NY: HarperCollins.

Social Services Committee (1990) *Community care: Carers*, Fifth report of Select Committee of House of Commons, London: HMSO.

Soper, K. and Trentmann, F. (2007) *Citizenship and consumption (consumption and public life)*, Basingstoke: Palgrave.

Spillman, B.C. (2004) 'Changes in elderly disability rates and the implications for health care utilization and cost', *Milbank Quarterly*, vol 82, no 1, pp 157-94.

Stearns, P.N. (1997) 'Stages of consumerism: recent work on the issues of periodization', *Journal of Modern History*, vol 69, no 1, pp 102-17.

Steinem, G. (1994) *Moving beyond words*, London: Bloomsbury.

Strauss, W. and Howe, N. (1992) *Generations: The history of America's future, 1584 to 2069*, New York, NY: William Morrow & Co.

Strauss, W. and Howe, N. (1997) *The fourth turning*, New York, NY: Broadway Books.

Strausser, S., McGovern, C. and Judt, M. (eds) (1998) *Getting and spending: European and American consumer societies in the 20th century*, Cambridge: Cambridge University Press.

Streeck, W. and Thelen, K. (2005) (eds) *Beyond continuity: Institutional change in advanced political economies*, Oxford: Oxford University Press.

Taylor, C. (2004) *Modern social imaginaries*, Durham, NC: Duke University.

Taylor, R. (2002a) 'Britain's world of work – myths and realities', ESRC Future of Work Programme (www.leeds.ac.uk/esrcfutureofwork/downloads/fow_publication_3.pdf, accessed 7 November 2007).

Taylor, R. (2002b) 'The diversity in Britain's labour market', ESRC Future of Work Programme (www.esrcsocietytoday.ac.uk/ESRCInfoCentre/Images/fow_publication_4_tcm6-6058.pdf, accessed 7 November 2007).

Taylor-Gooby, P.F. (1998) 'Choice and the policy agenda', in P. Taylor-Gooby (ed) *Choice and public policy: The limits to welfare markets*, Basingstoke: Macmillan.

Taylor-Gooby, P.F. (2002) 'The silver age of the welfare state: perspectives on resilience', *Journal of Social Policy*, vol 31, no 4, pp 597-622.

Thane, P. (2000) *Old age in English history*, Oxford: Oxford University Press.

Thane, P. (2003) 'Social histories of old age and aging', *Journal of Social History*, vol 37, no 1, pp 93-111.

Thomas, K., Nicholl, J. and Coleman, P. (2001) 'Use and expenditure on complementary medicine in England: a population based survey', *Complementary Therapies in Medicine*, vol 9, no 1, pp 2-11.

Tilly, C. (1984) *Big structures, large processes and huge comparisons*, New York, NY: Russell Sage Foundation.

Tilly, C. and Tilly, C. (1998) *Work under capitalism*, Oxford: Westview Press.

Timonen, V., Convery, J. and Cahill, S. (2006) 'Care revolution in the making? A comparison of cash-for-care programmes in four European countries', *Ageing & Society, vol 26*, no 3, pp 455-74.

Townsend, P. (1963) *The family life of old people*, Harmondsworth: Penguin Books.

Townsend, P. (1981) 'The structured dependency of the elderly', *Ageing & Society*, vol 1, no 1, pp 5-28.

Townsend, P. and Walker, A. (1995) *The future of pensions: Revitalising National Insurance*, Nottingham: European Labour Forum.

Townsend, P., Philimore, P. and Beattie, A. (1988) *Health and inequalities in the North*, London: Croom Helm.

Trentmann, F. (2004) 'Beyond consumerism: new historical perspectives on consumption', *Journal of Contemporary History*, vol 39, no 3, pp 373-401.

Turner, A., Drake, J. and Hills, J. (2004) *A new pension settlement for the twenty-first century: The second report of the Pensions Commission*, London: The Stationery Office. (www.pensionscommission.org.uk).

Turner, B.S. (1989) 'Ageing, politics and sociological theory', *British Journal of Sociology*, vol 40, no 4, pp 588-606.

Veblen, T. (1953) *The theory of the leisure class*, New York, NY: New American Library.

Victor, C.R. (1992) 'Do we need institutional care?', in F. Laczko and C.R.Victor (eds) *Social policy and elderly people*, Aldershot: Avebury, pp 259-75.

Vincent, J. (1999) 'Consumers, identity and old age', *Education and Ageing*, vol 14, no 2, pp 141-52.

Vincent, J. (2005) 'Understanding generations: political economy and culture in an ageing society', *British Journal of Sociology*, vol 56, no 4, pp 579-99.

Wacquant, L. (1989) 'Towards a reflexive sociology: A workshop with Pierre Bourdieu', *Sociological Theory*, vol 7, no 1, pp 26-63.

WAG (Welsh Assembly Government) (2003) *The Strategy for Older People in Wales*, Cardiff: WAG.

WAG (2006) *National Service Framework for Older People in Wales*, Cardiff: WAG.

Walker, A. (2006) 'Active ageing in employment: its meaning and potential', *Asia-Pacific Review*, vol 13, no 1, pp 78-93.

Walker, A. and Maltby, T. (1997) *Ageing Europe*, Buckingham: Open University Press.

Wallace, P. (1999) *Agequake: Riding the demographic rollercoaster shaking business, finance and our world*, London: Nicholas Brealey Publishing.

Wanless, D. (2006) *Securing good care for older people: Taking the long term view*, London: King's Fund.

Warde, A. (2002) 'Setting the scene: changing conceptions of consumption', in S. Miles, A. Anderson and K. Meethan (eds) *The changing consumer: Markets and meaning*, London: Routledge.

Warnes, A.M. (2006) 'The future life course, migration and old age', in J. Vincent, C. Phillipson and M. Downs (eds) *The futures of old age*, London: Sage Publications.

Warren, T. (2006) 'Moving beyond the gender wealth gap: on gender, class, ethnicity, and wealth inequalities in the United Kingdom', *Feminist Economics*, vol 12, nos 1-2, pp 195-219.

Webster, C. (1991) 'The elderly and the early National Health Service', in M. Pelling and R.M. Smith (eds) *Life, death and the elderly: Historical perspectives*, London: Routledge, pp 165-93.

Weiss, R.S. and Bass, S.A. (2002) 'Introduction', in R.S. Weiss and S.A. Bass (eds) *Challenges of the third age: Meaning and purpose in later life*, Oxford: Oxford University Press.

Wellman, B., Kelner, M. and Wigdor, B. (2001) 'Older adults' use of medical and alternative care', *Journal of Applied Gerontology*, vol 20, no 1, pp 3-23.

White, H. (1992) 'Succession and generations: looking back on chains of opportunity', in H.A. Becker (ed) *Dynamics of cohort and generations research*, Amsterdam: Thesis Publishers.

WHO (World Health Organization) (2002) *Active ageing: A policy framework document*, Geneva: WHO (http://whqlibdoc.who.int/hq/2002/WHO_NMH_NPH_02.8.pdf, accessed 10 December 2007).

Wiggins, R.D., Erzberger, C., Hyde, M., Higgs, P. and Blane, D. (2007) 'Optimal matching analysis using ideal types to describe the lifecourse: an illustration of how histories of work, partnership and housing relate to quality of life in early old age', *International Journal of Social Research Methodology*, vol 10, no 4, pp 259-78.

Willcocks, D., Peace, S. and Kellaher, L. (1987) *Private lives in public places*, London: Tavistock Publications.

Williams, R. (1983) *Keywords*, London: Fontana Press.

Yamada, A. (2002) *The evolving retirement income package: Trends in adequacy and equality in nine OECD Countries*, Labour Market and Social Policy Occasional Papers No 6063, Paris: Organisation for Economic Development and Co-operation.

Yang, Y. (in press) 'Long and happy: trends and patterns in happy life expectancy in the USA, 1970-2000', *Social Science Research*, (available online 21 September 2007, http://sociology.uchicago.edu/people/faculty/yang/Yang_SSR2007.pdf).

Young, M. and Schuller, T. (1991) *Life after work: The arrival of the ageless society*, London: HarperCollins.

Zaidi, A. and De Vos, K. (2002) *Income mobility of the elderly in Great Britain and the Netherlands: A comparative investigation*, SAGE Research Group Discussion Paper 9, London: London School of Economics.

Zaidi, A., Frick, J.R. and Buchel, F. (2005) 'Income mobility in old age in Britain and Germany', *Ageing & Society*, vol 25, no 4, pp 543-65.

Zukin, S. and Maguire, J.S. (2004) 'Consumers and consumption', *Annual Review of Sociology*, 30, no 1, pp 173-97.

Appendix: Methods and data

The findings presented in this book are based on a cross-sectional historical comparison of people at different ages, household types and income levels through a secondary analysis of Family Expenditure Survey of Great Britain (FES) data. (The Office for National Statistics (ONS) conducts the Northern Ireland Family Expenditure Survey, which is very similar to the FES. However, we did not include these data in our analyses). The data were taken from eight years of the FES at five-year intervals over the period 1968-2001. These data were accessed through the Economic and Social Data Service. The FES is a voluntary survey of a random sample of private households in the United Kingdom carried out by the ONS. The FES is primarily a survey of household expenditure on goods and services, as well as household income. The original purpose of the survey was to provide information on spending patterns for the purpose of calculating the Retail Price Index. The survey has been conducted annually since 1957, although since 1994, the survey reference period has changed from the calendar year to the financial year. Data collection is carried out throughout the year to avoid potential bias arising from seasonal variations in expenditures. Respondents maintain a detailed expenditure diary over 14 days to give indicators of their consumption patterns. In addition to expenditure and income data, the FES includes information on a range of socio-economic characteristics of the households (for example, composition, size, social class, occupation and age of the head of household).

The basic unit of the survey is the household, although data are collected at both household and individual level. The FES sample for Great Britain is drawn from the Small Users File of the Postcode Address File. From this, 672 postal sectors in Great Britain are randomly selected during the year after being arranged in strata defined by government office regions (sub-divided into metropolitan and non-metropolitan areas) and two 1991 Census variables – socio-economic group and ownership of cars. The sample size and response rates for each of the years included in these analyses are presented in Table A.1. On average, about 7,000 households are surveyed each year, representing an average response rate of 60%, although this has declined over the period covered in this book.

For the purpose of our analyses, households were divided according to the self-reported labour market status of the head of the household (HoH). In the FES, the head of the household is defined as follows. The HoH must be a member of the household and is, in order of precedence, the husband of the person or the person who either (a) owns the household accommodation, or (b) is legally responsible for the rent of the accommodation, or (c) has the household accommodation as an emolument or prerequisite, or (d) has the household accommodation by virtue of some relationship to the owner, lessee and so on who is not, himself, a member of the household. In the case of a married couple, where both are members of the household, the husband is the HoH, even if the wife owns the property. If

Table A.1: Number of households, response rate and labour market position of head of household in each year of the FES used

	1968	1973	1978	1983	1988	1993	1997/98	2000/01
Study characteristics								
Number of households	7,183	7,124	7,001	6,973	7,265	6,979	6,409	6,637
Response rate	63.01	62.49	61.41	61.17	63.73	61.22	56.22	58.22
Labour market position of the head of household								
Self-employed	7.14	6.91	6.20	7.30	9.55	9.03	8.18	8.09
Employed	68.22	65.30	61.19	51.28	49.21	44.98	48.15	48.70
Retired	13.92	15.79	17.70	20.28	24.36	38.92	39.41	25.61
Unemployed	10.72	12.00	14.91	21.14	16.88	7.08	4.26	17.60

Source: FES

the husband is not a member of the household, but the accommodation is in his name, his wife is the HoH. If two members of different sexes have equal claim, the male is to be taken as HoH. If two members of the same sex have equal claim, the older is taken as HoH. In each year, the HoH was asked to define their labour market position. In order to bring the FES classification of economic activity more into line with international definitions and other surveys, the range of options available have varied slightly over the years. For example, in 1968 respondents were asked to define themselves as one of the following: self-employed, a full-time employee at work, a part-time employee at work, a full-time employee away from work, a part-time employee away from work, retired or unoccupied. By 1983, a further distinction had been added to both the retired and unoccupied categories – namely, whether the respondent was above or below the minimum National Insurance pensionable age – and in 1993 the category of being on a 'work-related government training programme' was included. We identified four categories: those who identified themselves as self-employed, those who were in employment (both full- and part-time), those who were retired and those who were unemployed. The proportions in each of these categories are shown in Table A.1. However, for the purposes of these analyses, the self-employed were excluded as they are a particular and relatively small group, which makes it difficult to interpret their patterns of ownership of key goods.

At each year, the FES collected information about a range of goods owned by the household. An indication of the expansion of consumer culture in the UK over the time period is the growth in the number of variables in these household level datasets. In 1968, there were 571 variables, which increased to 1741 by 2001, reflecting the availability and importance of new goods on the market. For the purpose of our analyses, we selected those goods that were common to as many years as possible in order to explore changes over time. Household ownership of a telephone was recorded in each of the data years. Television ownership was recorded in all years apart from 1993. However, in 1988, the question changed from simply whether the household owned a television to how many televisions the household had. To maintain comparability over the time period, the responses in these latter waves were recoded into whether the household owned at least one television against households where there was no television. Whether the household owned a washing machine and whether the household owned a car were asked at each year from 1973 to 2001. In 1973 and 1978, respondents were asked whether the household owned a fridge or a freezer separately. However, from 1983 until 1997, respondents were asked whether they had a fridge, a fridge-freezer and/or a freezer. In order to maintain conceptual comparability across the waves, and to reflect the affordability of fridge-freezers from the 1980s, households that owned either a fridge or a fridge-freezer were combined. However, in 2001, this was changed again and fridge ownership was no longer an available option, although fridge-freezer was. As there was still a significant minority who owned fridges in 1997, this meant that responses were no longer comparable for this year and were excluded. We were also keen to find out about the ownership of new consumer goods resulting from technological advance. Given their more recent development, these variables were available for a much shorter time span and consequently their trajectories that much more truncated. From 1993, respondents were asked whether the household owned a video cassette recorder, a personal computer or a microwave oven. We also examined patterns of ownership and expenditure by equivalised income quintiles. We used the McClements Scale (Before Housing Costs) (McClements, 1977), as this is currently the most commonly used by the ONS.

Index

A

Abrams, M. 74
Abrams, Philip 2, 31
accumulated deprivation thesis 63
'active ageing' discourse 109-10, 112
active citizens *see* citizen consumers
advocacy organisations 101-2, 103, 104-5, 110, 111
'aestheticisation' of consumption 25
age
  age group division 29
  and consumption patterns 10, 50-60
    healthcare consumption 86, 87-93
    and household composition 43-7, 72-5
    and receipt of 'direct payments' 106
  see also generation
Age Concern 102, 103, 105
'age as leveller' hypothesis 63
ageing as problematic process 25-6
agency 26-7, 110, 114
  and third age 13, 14, 27, 39, 40
  see also citizen consumers
alternative therapies 81-2
Alzheimer's Society 102, 103, 105
Anderson, Benedict 34
Anderson, M. 5
Arber, S. 67
Audit Commission 100
Austen, Jane 15
autonomy *see* agency

B

baby-boomer cohorts 20, 37, 49, 82, 111
Ball, C. 16-17
Bass, S.A. 16
Bauman, Z. 25
Beck, U. 8
Becker, Henk 32
Blackburn, R. 1, 116
boundary setting and periodisation 22, 36-7
Bourdieu, Pierre 34, 35, 114
British Household Panel Surveys 62, 83
Brooker, C. 39

C

Calnan, M. 77
capitalism 3, 115-16
  global capitalism 114, 116-17
Capuzzo, P. 36
car ownership 56, 59, 72
  and gender 67-8, 73-4
carers and consumer voice 101-2
Carers National Association 105
Carers UK 102, 103, 105
Carnegie Inquiry 15
Casey, B. 68
categorisation of old age 6, 14-15, 16, 21
choice 25-6, 83, 116

'voice and choice' agenda 102-3, 104-5, 106, 108, 109, 112
chronic illness in later life 79
chronological periodisation 14-15, 16, 21
citizen consumers 11, 37, 46, 115
  devolution and policy 108-9, 112
  and New Labour modernisation 102-7
  voice 101-2, 104-5, 106
  and welfare state 75, 111, 116-19
Clarke, H. 95
class 6, 20
clothing expenditure 74
cohorts
  definition and use of term 29-30
    as distinct from 'generation' 30, 35-6
  and social change 29-40
    periodisation 22, 23-4*tab*
  and third age 20
collective identity *see* 'generational identity'
Commission for Social Care Inspection 110
commissioning care services 100-1
commodification 4, 25, 118
  healthcare 80-2, 109-11
community 20, 34
community care 99, 100-1
complementary and alternative medicines (CAMs) 81-2
computers *see* PC ownership
Comte, Auguste 31
Conservative governments 99-102
consumer capitalism 115-16
consumer citizenship *see* citizen consumers
Consumer Expenditure Survey (US) 66, 95
consumer movements 77-8
consumer society 4-8, 49-60, 114-16
consumerism
  periodisation 4-5, 22
  and reconstruction of later life 109-11
  and welfare 99-112
Consumers' Association 77
consumption
  association with youth 36, 49
  expenditure and household composition 43-7
    ownership of key consumer goods 44-7, 50-60, 64-75, 141-2
  income levels and consumption 61-75, 113
  and later life 1, 11, 49-60, 113
    contradictions of 114-16
  and social change 1, 4-8
  and third age 16, 25-7
  trends in 5, 9-10
Cook, F. 19
Corsten, Michael 32, 34
Counsel and Care 102, 105
couples *see* dual-pensioner households
cultural field
  and generation 32-6, 114, 115, 119
  of third age 14, 22, 25-6, 27, 47, 114